CW00539601

Diana Peacock is an accomplished and experienced family cook, who practises self-sufficiency. She is the author of *Good Home Baking*, *The Seasonal Cookbook*, *Grandma's Ways for Modern Days* and *How To Make Sweets and Treats*.

Also available

The Wildlife Garden
Healthy Eating for Life
How to Make Wines at Home
Soups for Every Season
How to Make Jams, Pickles and Preserves
Afternoon Tea
Foolproof Cakes

TRADITIONAL COUNTRY PRESERVING

Diana Peacock

ROBINSON

ROBINSON

Originally published in the UK in 2010 as *Good Home Preserving*, by Spring Hill, an imprint of How To Books

This edition published in Great Britain in 2014 by Robinson

Copyright © Diana Peacock 2010, 2014

The moral right of the author has been asserted.

All rights reserved.
No part of this publication may be reproduced, stored in a retrieval system, or transmitted, in any form, or by any means, without the prior permission in writing of the publisher, nor be otherwise circulated in any form of binding or cover other than that in which it is published and without a similar condition including this condition being imposed on the subsequent purchaser.

A CIP catalogue record for this book is available from the British Library.

ISBN 978-0-71602-371-5 (paperback)
ISBN 978-0-71602-378-4 (ebook)

Typeset in Great Britain by Ian Hughes – www.mousematdesign.com

Robinson
is an imprint of
Constable & Robinson Ltd
100 Victoria Embankment
London EC4Y 0DY

An Hachette UK Company
www.hachette.co.uk

www.constablerobinson.com

Contents

Introduction

The preservation of our food has been of the utmost importance to our survival for hundreds of years, to feed us through the bleak winter months in Great Britain. From freezing and drying to jams and pickling, all have helped keep food edible, when fresh has been scarce. Though we have shops well stocked with food and provisions that enable us not to have to worry about the shortages of winter time, when you grow your own fruit and vegetables for whatever reason, it is both sensible for the planet and your pocket to preserve the produce in the best possible way. Now we are able to freeze food effectively and reasonably economically it means we can have almost fresh-tasting fruit and vegetables all year round.

I find making my own jams and preserves both enjoyable and absorbing. Obviously it is very useful for using produce to its fullest and most productive, but it is also great fun.

Once you have mastered the art of making jams, chutneys and pickles, and it isn't difficult to do so, you can begin to experiment and make up your own recipes to suit your taste and whatever you may have a glut of at any one time.

Jams and other preserves make great presents and gifts at any time, but I have found them most welcome at Christmas when people are needing to entertain and tend to get through many preserves.

Never see preserving as a way to keep poor produce; it isn't worth it. All preserves need the best-quality fruit and vegetables; ripeness will be down to what is required for each individual type of preserve. For example, some jams are best prepared with under-ripe fruit, whereas the riper fruit is ideal for making jellies and syrups as the juice yield is higher.

Pride has always played an unashamed part in my preserve making, as I still get an inner glow when I say 'I made it myself', and hopefully you will get to feel this way about your own home-made preserves and thoroughly enjoy the process. It really is worthwhile.

1. Drying Fruit and Vegetables

Drying, along with salting, is one of the oldest known ways of preserving food. In hot climates it is also the most economical method. However, as we don't have a regular supply of sunshine available to us in Britain, it is better to dry produce indoors where a steady temperature can be maintained.

The two most important requirements for successful drying are a steady low temperature and ventilation. It is a lengthy process, but once the produce is ready to be dried it takes relatively little work to achieve a product that will keep for many months.

What do I need to dry my fruit and vegetables?

You can purchase electric drying machines that are economical to run and take all the worry out of the task. Depending on how much produce you wish to dry, you can choose from a range of prices from about £70 to £450. These machines come with full manufacturers' instructions.

Alternatively, you can use a conventional oven. This method will need more attention, but you can still achieve good results so long as you follow simple rules.

- Make sure your oven is available for many hours at a time as most foods take between 5 and 36 hours to dry out. They also require time to dry at room temperature before storing, so set aside a suitable space that is well ventilated and away from steam.
- The temperature needed to dry produce depends on what and how large the items are, but generally it is between 100–120°C/gas mark ½–1.
- Make a drying rack: take a cooling rack and stretch and secure a sheet of muslin over the top. The produce can be placed on top without touching to allow the warm air to pass around each piece.

Drying fruit

Stoned fruit – plums, peaches and apricots are all suitable. Place whole fruit on the prepared tray and leave to dry for 24–36 hours. Maintain the temperature until the skins have shrivelled. Leave for 12 hours in the air at room temperature to cool and allow any liquid to evaporate. Store in sterile jars.

Apples – peel, core and slice into 5mm thick rings. Dip the rings in a bowl of lightly salted water and thread onto bamboo canes that will fit into your oven, resting on the side ledges. Leave the door of the oven slightly open. Drying should take about 5 hours, and then leave in the air for 12 hours before packing into sterile jars.

Drying vegetables

Peas and beans can be placed on the drying rack after blanching them for 4 minutes and drying them on a tea towel. They may be dried in the oven or in an airing cupboard. It will take about 4 hours for peas and 6 for beans. Leave them for 1 hour in the air before packing them into clean jars.

Mushrooms can be hung in a warm dry place for 3–4 days, where they will dry out quite successfully. Use freshly picked large flat or open-cupped mushrooms and remove the stalks. Wipe the mushrooms clean with a cloth, thread them onto a string using a thick poultry needle and tie a knot between each mushroom. Hang up the strings and leave to dry out. Store the mushrooms in jars in a dark cupboard. I use these in soups, curries or omelettes.

Tomatoes can be dried on the rack in a very cool oven for 3–5 hours depending on the size. Cutting the tomatoes in half shortens the drying time but I think it spoils the flavour slightly.

2. *Freezing Fruit and Vegetables*

This is probably the method that preserves the most natural flavour, colour and appearance of produce. It is certainly the quickest and easiest method, needing few if any other ingredients to prolong the life of fruit and vegetables.

Most vegetables may be frozen after a little preparation and can be packaged in such a way as to enable you to lift the portions you need from the freezer at any one time. However, salad vegetables, such as lettuce and cucumbers, are unsuitable for freezing due to their high water content; once defrosted they would end up a mushy mess.

Fruit can be frozen successfully. It does become softer in texture when defrosted but is ideal for making jam. Some herbs may also be frozen for future use.

Packaging

Make sure the bags or containers you use are suitable for freezing. This is of the utmost importance to ensure there is no deterioration during the freezing time. Packaging must be thick enough not to tear easily as this will cause a loss of water and over time the flavour and quality of the produce will diminish.

Freezer bags

These are the cheapest and easiest packaging for freezing produce, and many brands include a white labelling area on each bag on which you can clearly label what is contained in the bag. They don't take up as much room as plastic containers and can hold oddly shaped, small or larger amounts depending on what suits you. As air takes up room and can spoil some frozen foods it is better to expel as much as possible before sealing the bags.

Plastic containers

These must have secure airtight lids and be labelled as suitable for freezing. Containers have the advantage of stacking well in the freezer and you can attach easily readable labels. They come in all shapes and sizes, so are suitable for freezing large or small amounts.

Glassware

Only use glass that's labelled as suitable for freezing; glass becomes more fragile once it's frozen and would make a complete mess of your freezer should it shatter inside it. If you are freezing produce in glass, wrap some foil or plastic around it just in case. The only things I tend to freeze in glass containers are stocks and ready-made preserves such as lemon curd.

Points to remember when freezing

To get the best out of your freezer:

- use the best produce, free from blemishes or squashy bits;
- freeze as soon after picking as possible;
- pack in meal-size amounts;
- cool all produce completely before packaging;
- exclude as much air from the packaging as you can;
- label and date the packages clearly;
- keep a notebook to record what's in your freezer and when it was frozen, so that you and your family can see immediately what is available to use. Cross out each item as it is used;
- keep your freezer well stocked; a fully stocked freezer uses less energy than an empty one;
- open the door only when necessary and for the shortest time possible.

Freezing fruit

Prepare the fruit for freezing as you would for cooking or making jams, hulling, topping and tailing, peeling and coring. The chart on pages 7–8 tells you exactly how to prepare each fruit.

There are five main ways to freeze fruit.

Sugar freezing – this is ideal for freezing fruit that you may wish to use for making jams or cooking in pies. It is good for soft fruits like raspberries and redcurrants. Freezer-safe lidded plastic containers are the best for this method.

(a) Wash the fruit and pat dry if necessary.
(b) Place the fruit in layers, sprinkling sugar over each layer. Allow about 150g sugar to every 500g fruit. Finish with a sprinkling of sugar.
(c) Make sure the contents fill the container as much as possible, leaving a little head space to allow for expansion, and press the lid down securely.
(d) Freeze immediately.

Syrup freezing – this is best for fruit that has little natural juice, such as peaches or grapes. Fruit that has a mild flavour retains it better if suspended in syrup while frozen. A syrup made from 600g sugar to 1 litre of water is suitable for most fruits. Heat the water in a large pan and stir in the sugar, continuing to stir until all the sugar has dissolved. Bring the syrup to the boil for 5 minutes then cool completely before using. Some fruit may need the addition of lemon juice or a vitamin C tablet dissolved in a tablespoon of warm water; this will stop them discolouring during freezing (see the chart on pages 7–8 for details).

Pack the washed fruit in rigid containers and pour over the cold syrup, leaving a gap of about 1.5cm between the fruit and the lid of the container. This gap allows for expansion during freezing. Crumple up a piece of greaseproof paper and place it on top of the fruit to keep it submerged before securing the lid firmly on top. You should find that 1 litre of syrup is sufficient to cover about 1.5kg fruit.

Dry freezing – this is the easiest method and is particularly suitable for soft fruits as no sugar has been used in their preparation, so you can use them for whatever you wish. Lay the washed fruit in a single layer on a freezable tray lined with silicone paper. If possible, try to avoid the fruits touching each other. Freeze for about 1½ hours until firm, and then pack in bags or containers.

Pre-poaching – this is suitable for firm-skinned fruits like plums and apricots as they become hard after freezing. Make a syrup using 400g sugar to 600ml water and boil for 5 minutes. Turn down the heat and add the prepared fruit, usually halved and stoned. Poach until just tender. Pack when cold and add some of the syrup to cover the fruit, as described above for syrup freezing.

Precooking – this is best for fruit that is very ripe and wouldn't withstand other methods of freezing. Wash the fruit and simmer in a little water until soft. You can add a bit of sugar at this stage if you like, or wait until after freezing and defrosting the fruit. Drain and pack into bags or containers when cool.

Thawing

Leave the fruit to defrost in the unopened container. Depending on the amount, it will take between 3 and 4 hours to defrost completely. I tend to get the pack out of the freezer the night before and put it in the fridge to thaw; it should be defrosted by the morning. If you are going to cook the fruit, it may be heated gently in a pan even if it is not thoroughly defrosted.

Storage times

All the methods will keep fruit fresh for about six months depending on your freezer.

Alphabetical guide to freezing fruit

Type of fruit	Method of freezing
Apples	1. Dry freeze without sugar. Peel, core and place in water with a squeeze of lemon juice. Drain, dry and freeze in plastic containers for best results. 2. In syrup, adding 1 tablespoon lemon juice to the syrup. 3. Precooking – ideal for using in pies and sauces.
Apricots	1. Sugar – blanch in boiling water for 1 minute before drying and layering with the sugar. 2. Syrup – cover with syrup, first adding 1 tablespoon lemon juice to the syrup. 3. Precooking – for use in pies and puddings.
Blackberries	All methods suitable.
Cherries	1. Dry freeze without sugar. Pour chilled water over the fruit and leave for 30 minutes. Dry well, stone if necessary. 2. Sugar freeze. 3. Syrup – add $1\frac{1}{2}$ tablespoons lemon juice to the syrup.
Black, red and white currants	All methods suitable.
Damsons	1. Syrup – add 2 tablespoons lemon juice or a vitamin C tablet to the syrup. 2. Precooking – for use in puddings, pies and fools.
Gooseberries	All methods suitable.
Grapes	Syrup – halve and remove the seeds or leave whole if seedless.
Peaches and nectarines, peeled or unpeeled	1. Sugar – halve and stone the fruit and prepare quickly as they soon lose their fresh colour. 2. Syrup – add $1\frac{1}{2}$ tablespoons lemon juice to the syrup. 3. Precooking – for use in puddings, pies and tarts.
Plums	1. Sugar – blanch in boiling water for 1 minute before drying and layering with sugar.

Plums continued	2. Syrup – first adding 1 tablespoon lemon juice to the syrup.
	3. Precooking – for use in pies and puddings.
Raspberries and strawberries	1. Dry freeze.
	2. Syrup – make a lighter syrup than above using 400g sugar
	to 1 litre water and use when cold.
	3. Sugar.
Rhubarb	All methods suitable. Prepare the rhubarb by washing and
	cutting into 2cm pieces. When dry freezing, blanch for 2 minutes
	in boiling water, drain and dry well.

Freezing vegetables

Generally this is much simpler than freezing fruit. The most important thing is to blanch the vegetables in boiling water before freezing them. This stops the vegetables from losing their colour, taste and nutritional value due to the action of enzymes on the produce.

Blanching

Blanch the vegetables in batches of no more than 500g. Use fresh boiling water for every different vegetable and for every 3kg of vegetables. For every litre of boiling water add 1 level teaspoon salt. Use a wire basket as you would for making chips; this makes life easier and stops some vegetables from being overblanched. Each vegetable has its own blanching time (see the chart on pages 9–10).

Lift the vegetables out and plunge them into chilled water; a bowl of cold water with ice cubes added is ideal. Drain and dry well with a clean tea towel; paper towel can get lodged in some vegetables. Pack in freezer bags or suitable plastic containers.

Storage times

Generally most well-prepared vegetables will keep for 4 to 10 months. See the chart for storage times for each vegetable.

Cooking times

See the chart for approximate cooking times for each vegetable.

Alphabetical guide to freezing vegetables

The cooking times given below are a guide only. Cook for more or less time according to your own taste.

Type of vegetable	Preparation	Blanching/storage/ cooking times
Aubergines	Cut into slices	4 minutes/10 months/from frozen 5 minutes
Broad beans	Remove from pods and use similar-sized beans for blanching	3 minutes/10 months/ from frozen 7 minutes
French beans	Top and tail	2 minutes/10 months/from frozen 6 minutes
Runner beans	String and top and tail, slice into 1–2cm pieces	2 minutes/10 months/from frozen 6 minutes
Beetroot	Use whole small beetroots, wash without breaking the skins	No blanching, just boil until tender and cool/8 months
Broccoli	Divide into fairly even-sized florets	4 minutes/10 months/from frozen 6 minutes
Brussels sprouts	Remove any loose leaves	3–4 minutes depending on size/10 months/from frozen 8 minutes
Cabbages, red and green types	Remove large outer leaves if damaged and shred	2 minutes/6 months/from frozen 7 minutes
Carrots	If young just trim off the top; older ones, scrub and slice or dice	4 minutes/10 months/from frozen 8 minutes
Cauliflower	Divide into even-sized florets	3 minutes/6 months/from frozen 8 minutes
Courgettes	Trim the ends and slice thickly	1 minute/8 months/thaw for 30 minutes, fry until cooked

Fennel	Trim off the roots and cut into 3–4cm pieces	3 minutes/6 months/from frozen until tender
Leeks	Cut into 2cm slices	2 minutes/6 months/thaw in the container and fry as necessary
Mushrooms	Cut large ones into thick slices, leave small ones whole. Fry lightly before cooling and freezing	No blanching/3 months/thaw before cooking
Parsnips	Peel and cut into 1cm slices	2 minutes/10 months/from frozen best roasted for 15–20 minutes or used in soups
Peas and mangetout	Pod and grade into small, medium and large peas and mangetout	Peas 1–2 minutes, mangetout 3 minutes/10 months/from frozen 4–7 minutes
Spinach	Wash in cold water	1 minute/10 months/from frozen 2–3 minutes
Sweet peppers	Cut in half, deseed and cut into strips	2 minutes/6 months/from frozen, fry for soups, curries, stews etc.
Tomatoes	May be frozen whole but best puréed or juiced	No blanching/6 months/thaw all types completely before using
Turnips and swedes	Peel and dice	2 minutes/8 months/from frozen 7–8 minutes

Freezing herbs

I tend to freeze herbs like basil, chives, mint, tarragon and parsley and any others that die away during the winter months. Thyme and rosemary are with us all year round so I don't see the point of freezing them.

Wash and dry them well and place them in freezer bags in small quantities. Push out as much of the air as you can, then secure the bag and freeze immediately. Once thawed, the herbs wilt, so they are only suitable for cooking with. Use all herbs from frozen.

Another way of freezing them is to chop the herbs or, in the case of basil, tear them into small pieces and put them in the sections of an ice-cube tray. Pour a little water over and freeze immediately. When you want to use your herbs, simply add the frozen cube to the pan and the water will melt. This gives the herbs an excellent fresh flavour.

3. Preparing for Preserving

Making your own jams, chutneys, pickles and all the other wonderful preserves is a very satisfying and worthwhile occupation. Once you have mastered the basic routines you can begin to use your imagination and create your own recipes.

Because preserves are often cooked with sugar and or vinegar, many have a long shelf life and also make excellent gifts for family and friends. However, there are a few important rules you must remember to ensure your preserves don't spoil during storage.

Rules for successful preserving

- Always use fruit and vegetables that are unspoilt. Ripeness will depend on the recipe as some need under-ripe produce whereas others, like fruit syrups, are best prepared with ripe fruits.
- Wash all the fruit and vegetables well in cold water, remove any debris with a clean sponge-type scourer if necessary, but always be careful not to break the skins or peel.
- Always sterilise all jars and their lids and any other equipment that you may need to use (see 'How to sterilise the jars' on page 15). This is most important: the whole point of preserving food in this way is to extend the life of the produce, but this can only happen when the organisms that cause food to spoil are destroyed and no others are introduced during packing.
- Keep work surfaces spotlessly clean around where you are working to make sure that all possible contamination of the preserves is kept to a minimum.
- Always label and date the jars; this way you will be able to see clearly what is contained in them and how long ago it was made. This is especially important if you make lots of different types of preserve because they can end up looking very similar on the shelf.
- Before you begin, always read through the relevant instructions

and recipes for whatever you wish to make, and ensure you have all your ingredients and equipment to hand before starting.

- If you don't have a pantry or cool dark cupboard in which to store your preserves, put them in lidded plastic boxes and store them in an outdoor shed or as a last resort in the fridge. They must be kept away from direct heat and light to preserve their freshness.

Specialist equipment for preserving

You will probably already have most of the basic utensils for preserving, but there are some specialist products that I would advise you to invest in to help make life easier. These are listed below.

A preserving or maslin pan is a specially made pan with a handle and a lip for ease of pouring. It is a wide-necked heavy-based pan that allows your preserves to cook evenly and quickly. The most popular size usually holds about 9 litres, though you can get smaller and larger ones if necessary. They cost upwards of £25 but will last for a long time. I would advise you to buy a stainless steel one as they can be used for all preserving methods, whereas other metals such as copper do not react well to vinegar and they cost four or five times more than stainless steel. You can also use your maslin pan to make toffee and fudge and for any other recipes that call for a heavy-based pan.

A wide-necked preserving or jam funnel is useful when it's time to fill your jars. It minimises spillage and gets the preserve in the jar quicker, stopping the air from getting to the preserve for any length of time.

A jam thermometer takes all the guesswork out of cooking times. You will know at a reading of the thermometer when jams and jellies are ready to test for the setting point. It is still advisable to test manually just to make sure, but using a thermometer means you don't have to keep checking over and over again.

A **jelly or preserving bag** is a must for making jellies and fruit syrups as they usually come with a stand to keep the bag stable while you are straining the fruit. Usually made from nylon or fine plastic, they are easy to wash and are reusable.

Other basic equipment

A long-handled wooden spoon is essential for stirring the preserves while they are cooking, as the contents of the pan get incredibly hot and boiling sugar causes terrible burning of the skin. So, even using a long-handled spoon, always take great care when you are stirring a pan full of boiling sugar.

Accurate kitchen scales for measuring sugar and other ingredients.

A heatproof jug for measuring juices when making jelly and syrups.

A ladle used with a funnel makes filling jam jars and bottles very easy and safe.

Pieces of muslin cloth can be made into small bags to hold pips, pith or whole spices during marmalade or pickling processes.

Large bowls to hold juices, fruit and any other ingredients. I find I need at least two large and several smaller ones for different jobs.

Teaspoons, dessertspoons and tablespoons are all necessary for measuring and mixing.

Jars and bottles with well-fitting lids – jars that have screw tops are best and easiest to use and sterilise. I tend to reuse jam and marmalade jars from bought products, though you can buy empty jars if you wish. Build up a good collection of varying sizes from 150ml to 1 litre-sized jars. Kilner-type jars are useful for storing dried produce.

Labels – plain white sticky labels are ideal for your everyday preserves or you can buy decorated ones in the shops. I find a permanent marker pen is best for writing on the labels, but if you have a computer why not have a go at designing and printing your own labels? It's amazing how professional they look.

Fancy covers – cloth and paper covers look lovely on preserves intended as gifts, but keep them for decoration only. To ensure the life and freshness of your preserves, always use a good lid. You can use waxed discs and cloth covers if you tie them securely, but when it comes time to eat the preserves the cloth lids are more of a nuisance than anything.

How to sterilise the jars

It is of the utmost importance that all jars and lids are completely sterile before using them to store your preserves. They can be easily contaminated from a small amount of bacteria in the nooks and crannies of jars, but lids are particularly bad for this.

You can sterilise the jars by heating them in a microwave or conventional oven or, if you prefer, you can use a sterilising solution such as Milton.

Whichever method you choose, first wash the jars and lids in hot soapy water and rinse them well in hot water.

Using a microwave

Pour a little hot water into each jar, place in the microwave and heat on full power for 45 seconds for one jar or 1 minute if you are doing two at a time.

Using a conventional oven

Put the jars on a baking sheet and place in a cold oven. Set the oven temperature to 150°C/gas mark 2 for 20 minutes.

Using a sterilising solution

Use a solution such as Milton just as you would with baby feeding equipment. Follow the manufacturer's instructions on the solution strength. I find this the best and easiest method. I use a large washing-up bowl specifically for this job. Plastic lids can also be sterilised in this way.

Sterilising the lids

To sterilise metal lids simply place them in a pan of hot water, bring to the boil and then simmer for 10 minutes. Allow the lids to remain in the water until needed.

Essential ingredients for preserving

The produce

All fruit and vegetables should be of good quality. Just one piece with the smallest amount of contamination can cause a whole batch of preserve to be spoilt. Usually it is the flavour and shelf life that are affected.

Sugar

This is an obvious ingredient in most preserves. You will find full details with each recipe of the type and amount of sugar needed.

Pectin

Pectin is the setting or thickening agent used in jam- and preserve-making. It is particularly important in jam, jelly and marmalade preparation. It is a complex carbohydrate found in and between the cell walls of plants and is what keeps them rigid. As fruit ages and ripens pectin is lost, causing older, riper fruits to go soft and limp.

Most fruit contains some pectin in its structure but in varying degrees according to the fruit. This is why we sometimes need to add pectin with the sugar in our jam-making.

Pectin can be bought in the shops or made at home. Commercial pectin is usually in powdered form and in measured sachets. Read the manufacturer's instructions for use. The amount needed is usually 1 x 13g sachet for every kilo of fruit. It is always better to use less rather than more pectin, as a softer-set jam is far more acceptable than a stiff, unusable one. Incidentally, pectin is believed to be beneficial for those with digestive problems.

Home-made Pectin Stock

This is made from fruit very rich in pectin and is used in liquid form. It is usually added just before the sugar. Use under-ripe fruit that is still very firm for the best possible yield.

Makes about 1.2 litres
1.5kg cooking apples, gooseberries and redcurrants
(use any or all of the fruits)
600ml water

Use 100ml of pectin stock instead of 1x13g sachet of pectin.

1. Place the fruit in a pan with the water and bring to the boil. Then reduce the heat and simmer for about 30 minutes until everything is pulpy and juicy.

2. Strain through a jelly bag, or a piece of muslin folded in two, into a bowl and return the pulp to the pan.

3. Add 300ml water to the pan, stir and leave to stand for 1 hour.

4. Bring back to simmering and cook gently for 45–50 minutes.

5. Strain the juice as before.

6. Put both sets of juice in a pan and boil for 5 minutes.

7. Store in sterilised bottles or jars.

Guide to pectin content of fruits

High pectin content	Medium pectin content	Low pectin content
Blackcurrants	Apricots	Late-picked blackberries
Citrus fruit	Early-picked blackberries	Cherries
Cooking apples	Greengages	Dessert apples
Cranberries	Rhubarb	Peaches
Damsons	Raspberries, just ripe	Pears
Gooseberries		Strawberries
Under-ripe plums		

Why do I need to add lemon juice?

This is a necessary ingredient in ensuring the preserves set well. Combined with the pectin during cooking, it thickens the jam. Some commercially produced jams contain citric acid, but lemon juice is easy and available to use for home-made preserves.

4. Making Jams

Making jam is a wonderful way to preserve the flavours of fruit for the winter months.

The Basic Method

Each recipe will be specific about water, sugar, lemon juice and pectin content. Cooking times will also be given but will be very approximate, so use them as a guide only.

1. Prepare the fruit by washing thoroughly and topping and tailing stalks and bits of leaves. Discard any poor-quality fruit; good jam cannot be made from bad fruit. When chopping or cutting up the fruit, particularly juicy fruit like peaches, do so in a bowl so that you can catch all the juice and add it to the pan. If you like a smoother texture to your jam, cut your fruit into smaller pieces or chop it in the food processor, but remember the fruit will take less time to cook.

2. Cook the fruit, adding water as necessary. Some fruits need plenty of water and some need none. Lemon juice is also added at this stage if the fruits lack acid content. Some of the recipes need the fruit to begin to fall; this simply means they begin to pulp and go very soft.

3. Add the sugar. The sugar used in all the recipes is simple white granulated sugar. Some people find it useful to warm it first in an oven for 5–10 minutes at 160°C/gas mark 2. This does speed up the time required for dissolving the sugar. Stir the mixture constantly over a medium heat until the sugar has dissolved. Check the back of the spoon for sugar crystals; there should be no sign of these when it has all dissolved. This is the time to add any pectin being used. The recipe will tell you if you need this.

4. Bring to the boil until a setting point is reached; an average time for this will be given in the recipe. If a scum forms on the top of the bubbling mixture add half a teaspoon butter and it will disperse as you stir.

5. Test for setting point. When you are an experienced jam-maker you will be able to tell when it has reached setting point, but the test must still be done to make sure. The consistency thickens and becomes gel-like and more translucent. Have a cold saucer ready (keep this in the fridge or in very cold water until needed). Drop a small amount of jam onto the saucer, allow it to cool for a few seconds and then push it with your finger. If it is ready it should wrinkle and stay in place; it may move a little but should not run round your finger.

6. Some jams are best left to cool for 5–15 minutes depending on which fruit is used. Then stir before potting. This helps to distribute the fruit evenly through the jam.

7. Use a jam funnel to help you ladle the jam into the sterile jars and secure the lid of each jar.

8. Label and date your jam when cool for future reference.

9. Store all unopened jars in a cool dark place and once open keep in the fridge and use within 1 month.

A note about the recipes

Most of the jams should keep for up to a year unopened. Lower sugar jams will keep for less time but this is indicated in the recipe.

Prepare all the fruit as instructed in Chapter 3, 'Preparing for Preserving', unless otherwise stated in the recipes.

Apple Jam

To make larger quantities of this jam, for every extra 500g of apples add an extra 500g sugar, 200ml water and the juice of half a lemon.

MAKES ABOUT 5 X 500G JARS

About 1.5kg cooking apples (Bramleys are ideal)
600ml water
Juice of 2 lemons
1.5kg sugar

1. Peel, core and dice the apples and place in a pan with the water and lemon juice. Put the apple peel and cores in a muslin bag and add to the pan. This helps the jam to set.

2. Bring to the boil then simmer until the apples are soft and pulpy. Use tongs to lift out and squeeze the muslin bag. Discard the bag of peel.

3. Add the sugar and stir over a medium heat until the sugar has dissolved.

4. Bring to the boil and boil for 5 minutes then test for setting.

5. Allow to stand for 3 minutes then ladle into prepared jars. Secure the lids well.

6. Label and date the jars when cool.

Variation
Add a small piece of cinnamon stick or a teaspoon of ground cinnamon to the apples at the start of cooking. Remove the stick before adding the sugar.

Apricot Jam

MAKES ABOUT 6 X 500G JARS

2kg fresh apricots
300ml water
Juice of 1 lemon
2kg sugar
1 x 13g sachet pectin or 100ml pectin stock

1. Wash, halve and stone the fruit. Keep about 8 of the stones for cooking with the jam; this adds to the flavour of the finished jam. If you prefer a smoother jam, quarter the fruit.

2. Place the fruit, stones and water in a pan and bring to the boil then add the lemon juice and simmer until the fruit is tender. If you like smaller pieces of fruit in your jam, cook for longer until the apricots are very soft. Remove the stones.

3. Stir in the sugar and the pectin and continue stirring until the sugar has dissolved.

4. Bring the mixture to the boil, stirring occasionally, and boil for 5 minutes. Remove from the heat while you test for setting. If the jam is not ready, continue boiling for 1 more minute and test again.

5. When the jam is ready, allow it to stand for 5 minutes then stir and ladle into prepared jars. Secure the lids and label the jars when cool.

Blackberry Jam

MAKES ABOUT 8 X 500G JARS

3kg blackberries
200ml water
Juice of 2 lemons
3kg sugar
2 x 13g sachets of pectin or 200ml pectin stock, if you prefer a firmer set

1. Place the fruit and water in a large pan and bring to the boil, then stir in the lemon juice and simmer until the fruit is tender.

2. Add the sugar and pectin if using and continue to simmer, stirring the mixture until the sugar has dissolved.

3. Bring the jam to the boil, stirring occasionally. Then boil rapidly for 5 minutes and test for setting point. This will occur more quickly if you have added pectin.

4. Allow the jam to cool for 5 minutes then stir to distribute the fruit evenly and ladle into sterile jars.

5. Seal, label and date the jars when cool.

Blackberry and Apple Jam

Makes about 8 x 500g jars

1kg cooking apples
2kg blackberries
280ml water
Juice of 2 lemons
3kg sugar

1. Cook the apples with half of the water and the lemon juice for 5 minutes then add the blackberries and the rest of the water. Continue to simmer until the fruit is tender.

2. Stir in the sugar and allow to dissolve.

3. Bring the jam to the boil and boil rapidly for 10 minutes then check for the setting point.

4. Allow to cool for 5 minutes then stir and ladle into sterile jars.

5. Seal the jars and label and date them when cool.

Blackberry and Elderberry Jam

Collect the fruit as soon as they are ripe if they are from the wild as the pectin content is higher. Alternatively, a 13g sachet of pectin added to the fruit with the sugar will help with the setting.

MAKES ABOUT 7 X 500G JARS

1kg blackberries
1kg elderberries
180ml water
Juice of 1 lemon
1.75kg sugar

1. Wash the fruit, remove any bits of blackberry stalk and use a fork to remove the fruit from the elderberry stems.

2. Put the blackberries and water in a pan and simmer for 3–4 minutes then add the elderberries and lemon juice and continue to simmer for another 10 minutes.

3. Add the sugar while the fruit is still on a low heat and stir until the sugar is completely dissolved.

4. Bring the mixture to the boil and continue to boil for 8 minutes then test for setting point.

5. When the jam is ready, allow it to cool for 5 minutes then ladle into prepared jars.

6. Label and date the jars when cool.

Blackcurrant Jam

MAKES ABOUT 8 X 500G JARS

2kg blackcurrants
1.2 litres water
2.5kg sugar

1. Put the fruit and water into the pan and bring to the boil, stirring continuously.

2. Reduce the heat and allow to simmer for 30 minutes or until the fruit is tender and beginning to burst.

3. Stir in the sugar over a very low heat and allow to dissolve thoroughly.

4. Bring the mixture to the boil, stirring gently. Continue to boil vigorously for 5 minutes then check for setting point. Boil again if necessary until setting point is reached.

5. Allow to cool for 5 minutes, stir, then ladle into sterile jars.

6. Seal the jars and label and date them when cool.

Variation
Add 1 teaspoon of vanilla extract after the setting point is reached. Stir it thoroughly into the jam before potting.

Blueberry Jam

MAKES ABOUT 2 X 450G JARS

500g blueberries
100ml water
Juice of 1 lemon
450g sugar

1. Put the fruit, water and lemon juice in a pan and simmer for 8–10 minutes or until the fruit is tender.

2. Add the sugar and stir over a low heat until it has dissolved.

3. Bring the mixture to the boil and continue boiling for about 25 minutes.

4. Remove from the heat and test for setting point.

5. Allow the jam to stand for 10 minutes before potting and sealing.

6. Label and date the jars when cool.

Variation
To give a bit of extra flavour, add a bay leaf to the fruit at the first stage of cooking and remove it before adding the sugar.

Storage
This should keep for up to 9 months unopened.

Cherry Jam

MAKES ABOUT 4 X 450G JARS

1.5kg cherries
Juice of 2 lemons
1 x 13g sachet pectin
1.25kg sugar

1. Wash and remove the stones from the cherries. Put about 10 of the stones in a muslin bag.

2. Put the cherries, lemon juice and the bag of stones in a pan and simmer for about 30 minutes until the cherries are just tender.

3. Turn down the heat. Remove the bag of stones, add the pectin and stir in the sugar. Continue to stir over a low heat until the sugar has dissolved.

4. Bring the mixture to the boil and boil for 5 minutes. Remove from the heat and test for setting.

5. When the jam is ready, allow it to cool for 10 minutes, then stir and ladle into prepared jars.

6. Seal the jars and label when cool.

Variations
To make a smoother jam, chop the cherries before simmering them. They will also take less time to cook. To add flavour and piquancy, add 1–2 tablespoons of rum and stir into the jam just before potting.

Storage
This should keep for up to 9 months unopened.

Damson Jam

2.5kg damsons
800ml water
3kg sugar

1. Wash the fruit. The damsons may be cooked with or without the stones. I prefer to cook them without so I always cut the fruit in half and remove the stones. They also cook faster without them. But, if you wish, leave the fruit whole and the stones will start to float to the top as the mixture boils so you can skim them off.

2. Put the fruit in the pan with the water and simmer gently until tender. This will take about 20 minutes if the damsons are whole or 12–15 minutes if stoned.

3. Keep the fruit on a low heat, add the sugar and stir until it dissolves completely. Bring the mixture to the boil and boil steadily for about 10 minutes then test for setting point.

4. Leave to stand for 5 minutes, then stir and ladle into prepared jars.

5. Label and date the jars when cool.

Dessert Apple Jam

MAKES ABOUT 4 X 500G JARS

1.5kg apples, any variety
Zest and juice of 1 large lemon
200ml water
1.25kg sugar

1. Put the water in the pan and add the zest and juice of the lemon.

2. Peel, core and dice the apples, placing them in the water and lemon juice as you prepare each one. Stir to coat the apples. This will stop them discolouring.

3. Bring the apple mixture to the boil then simmer for 8–10 minutes until the fruit is soft.

4. Stir in the sugar and continue to stir over a low heat until all the sugar has dissolved.

5. Bring the mixture to the boil and boil vigorously for 8 minutes then test for setting point.

6. Cool for 5 minutes, stir and ladle into prepared jars.

7. Label and date the jars when cool.

Variation
As you add the sugar, sprinkle in 1 level teaspoon of ground cinnamon and a large pinch of freshly grated nutmeg.

Storage
This should keep for up to 9 months unopened.

Elderberry Jam

Fruit that's just ripe is best for this jam as it contains the most pectin. If you are in any doubt, add 1 x 13g sachet of pectin to the fruit when you add the sugar.

MAKES ABOUT 6 X 500G JARS

1.5kg elderberries
250ml water
Juice of 1 lemon
1.75kg sugar

1. Wash the fruit. Remove the berries from the stems using a fork and place in the pan with the water and lemon juice.

2. Bring to simmering point and cook gently for about 8 minutes.

3. Add the sugar and pectin if using and stir until all the sugar has dissolved.

4. Bring to the boil and boil vigorously for 6–7 minutes then test for setting. Continue to boil if necessary for another 2 minutes and test again. If you have added pectin the jam will set more quickly.

5. Allow the jam to stand for 5 minutes, then stir and ladle into prepared jars.

6. Label and date the jars when cool.

Gooseberry Jam

If you are picking your own gooseberries, use berries that are still firm and not quite ripe. Don't worry if the odd ripe one is used so long as the majority are under-ripe. Gooseberries at this stage are at their optimum pectin content.

MAKES ABOUT 9 X 500G JARS

2.25kg gooseberries
800ml water
2.5kg sugar

1. Wash and top and tail the gooseberries. Place in the pan with the water and bring to the boil. Then simmer until the berries begin to pop open and release the juice; this will take about 15 minutes.

2. Turn the heat right down and add the sugar. Stir until it is completely dissolved.

3. Bring the mixture to the boil and boil for 10–15 minutes then test for setting.

4. Allow to cool for 5 minutes then stir and ladle the jam into prepared jars.

5. Label and date the jars when cool.

Gooseberry and Elderflower Jam

If you like just a hint of elderflower flavour use 2 heads;
for a concentrated flavour use 4.

MAKES ABOUT 8 X 550G JARS

2–4 elderflower heads, washed
1 litre water
2kg gooseberries, topped and tailed and washed
2.25kg sugar

1. Put the flowers in a pan with the water and bring to the boil then simmer for 15 minutes. Leave the flowers in the water and allow the liquid to cool. When it is completely cold, strain the water into a measuring jug until you reach the 750ml mark. Top up with cold water if necessary.

2. Put the gooseberries in the pan with the elderflower water and bring to the boil then simmer until the gooseberries are tender and beginning to pop.

3. Stir in the sugar and continue stirring until the sugar has completely dissolved.

4. Bring to the boil and boil for 10 minutes then test for setting.

5. When the jam is ready, allow it to cool for 5 minutes then stir and ladle into prepared jars.

6. Label and date the jars when they are cool.

Grape Jam

Because many recipes require grapes to be skinned, I decided to process my grapes whole, with the skins on, until they were reduced almost to a purée. But I kept back about 10 grapes and halved these. This gives the jam texture and also the skins help the jam to set. I used half green and half black grapes. They will each have a different setting point so it is impossible to give precise timings.

MAKES ABOUT 5 X 500G JARS

2kg grapes
Juice of 1 lemon
250ml water
1.25kg sugar

1. Prepare your grapes by washing well to rid them of any yeasts and either use a food processor or chop them by hand. Leave a few fairly large pieces to your own taste.

2. Put them in a pan over a low heat and add the lemon juice and water. Cook for 5–10 minutes depending on the size of the pieces.

3. Add the sugar and stir until all the sugar has dissolved.

4. Bring to the boil and continue to boil for about 5 minutes before testing for setting.

5. Allow to cool for 10 minutes then stir and ladle into the prepared jars.

6. Label and date the jars when they are cool.

Storage
This should keep for up to 6 months unopened.

Greengage Jam

Greengages are green plums. They have a delicious honey flavour and make wonderful jam.

MAKES ABOUT 6 X 500G JARS

1.5kg greengages
270ml water
1.5kg sugar

1. Wash the fruit and halve it. Remove the stones. Place the fruit and water in a pan, bring to the boil and then simmer for 15–20 minutes or until the fruit is very tender.

2. Add the sugar and stir until the sugar has completely dissolved. Do this over a low heat.

3. Bring the mixture to the boil and boil for 10 minutes then test for setting.

4. Allow to cool for 10 minutes then stir the jam and ladle it into prepared jars.

5. Label and date the jars when cool.

Hedgerow Jam

This is a classic British jam made from our autumnal delights,
fruits, berries and even nuts. You will need a fine nylon or plastic
sieve or jelly bag for this as the fruits contain lots of bits and pieces
that need to be removed before you can use them for jam.

MAKES ABOUT 7 X 500G JARS

1.5kg mixture of crab apples, haws, rose hips, sloes, rowan berries
1kg mixture blackberries and elderberries
100g hazelnuts, finely chopped
About 500ml water
1kg sugar plus extra (see method for exact weight)

1. Wash all the fruit well and add the crab apples, haws, rose hips,
sloes and rowan berries to the pan. Just cover with the water; use
more or less than 500ml as necessary. Simmer until the fruits are soft
and mushy. Mash them with a potato masher.

2. Sieve the pulp into a clean bowl, pushing as much of the pulp
through the sieve as possible but retaining the seeds and other bits.
Discard what is left in the sieve.

3. Weigh the pulp and weigh out the equivalent amount of sugar.

4. Put the pulp, blackberries and elderberries in a pan and simmer
for 10 minutes until the blackberries and elderberries are tender.

5. Stir in the hazelnuts.

6. Stir in the 1kg of sugar plus the amount to match the weight of the pulp and continue stirring until all the sugar has dissolved.

7. Bring the mixture to the boil and boil vigorously for about 10 minutes, then test for setting.

8. Leave to cool for 5 minutes, stir well and ladle the jam into prepared jars.

9. Label and date the jars when cool.

Storage
This should keep for up to 9 months unopened.

High Dumpsy Dearie Jam

This unusual-sounding jam comes from Worcestershire, but the origins of the name remain a mystery to me. It is a recipe that uses up the last of the autumnal fruits from the orchard: apples, plums and pears. As it is made with a combination of fruits, it doesn't really matter how much you have of one kind of fruit so long as it all weighs about 3kg.

MAKES ABOUT 8 X 500G JARS

3kg apples, plums and pears
150ml water, slightly more if necessary
2cm (approximately) piece of root ginger, tied in a muslin bag
Grated zest and juice of 1 lemon
2kg sugar

1. Peel, core and slice the apples and pears. Halve and stone the plums. Put the fruit in a pan with the water. Bring to the boil, turn down the heat and simmer for about 20–30 minutes. Halfway through the cooking time, add the ginger and lemon zest and juice. Add more water to the fruit if it looks too dry.

2. Remove the pan from the heat and stir in the sugar. Return the pan to a very low heat and continue stirring until all the sugar has dissolved.

3. Bring the mixture to the boil then boil until a setting point is reached. This will take between 10 and 20 minutes. Don't overboil the jam, however, as you will lose some of the flavour.

4. Leave the jam to cool for 5 minutes then stir it and ladle into prepared jars.

5. Label and date the jars when cool.

Storage
This should keep for up to 9 months unopened.

Mango Jam

There are two ways of preparing this jam: the first method requires precooking, the second needs no precooking but the fruit must be prepared the day before you make the jam and left to stand overnight.

MAKES ABOUT 3 X 500G JARS

200ml water
Juice of 1 large or 2 small limes
1.25kg just ripe mangoes
750g sugar
1 tsp vanilla extract

Precooking method
1. Place the water and lime juice in a pan.

2. Peel and slice the mangoes quite thinly or cut into small cubes and place in the water, adding as much of the mango juice as you can.

3. Simmer for 10–15 minutes until the fruit is soft.

4. Stir in the sugar over a low heat and continue stirring until all the sugar has dissolved.

5. Stir in the vanilla extract and bring the mixture to the boil. Boil vigorously for about 20 minutes then test for setting. It won't be a firm set.

6. Allow the jam to cool for 5 minutes then stir and ladle into prepared jars.

7. Label and date the jars when they are cool.

No precooking method

1. Place the prepared fruit in a pan. Combine the water and lime juice and pour over the fruit. Pour over the sugar, cover and leave to stand overnight.

2. The next day add the vanilla extract and bring the mixture slowly to the boil, stirring to dissolve any sugar crystals.

3. Boil vigorously for about 40 minutes then test for setting point.

4. Allow the jam to cool for 5 minutes then stir and ladle into prepared jars.

5. Label and date the jars when they are cool.

Storage
Whichever method of preparation you choose, this jam should keep for up to 6 months unopened.

Mulberry Jam

Mulberries are not easy to come by but, if you are lucky enough to get some, they make wonderful jam – this is definitely one of my favourites.

MAKES ABOUT 3 X 500G JARS

1kg mulberries
1 large Bramley apple
100ml water
Juice of 1 lemon
1kg sugar

1. Wash and hull the mulberries and peel, core and dice the apple. Place them in the pan with the water and lemon juice.

2. Simmer for about 10 minutes or until the apple begins to fall or pulp.

3. Remove from the heat and stir in the sugar. Continue stirring until the sugar has dissolved.

4. Bring the mixture to the boil and boil for 15 minutes then test for setting.

5. Leave to cool for 10 minutes then stir the jam and ladle into prepared jars.

6. Label and date the jars when they are cool.

Peach Jam

You may peel the peaches if you prefer not to have
any skin in your jam.

MAKES ABOUT 5 X 500G JARS

2kg ripe but firm peaches
2 large lemons
250ml water
1.75kg sugar

1. Cut the peaches in half and remove the stones. Remove the kernel from each stone and crack them to release the flavour during cooking. Chop the peaches into chunks and place in a pan with the kernels and any juice that has escaped.

2. Cut the lemons in half and add the juice to the pan. Place the lemon skins in the pan with the peaches and pour over the water.

3. Bring to the boil then simmer for about 10 minutes or until the peaches are soft.

4. Use tongs to squeeze out the juice from the lemon skins and discard.

5. Remove the pan from the heat and turn the heat down low. Stir in the sugar.

6. Return the pan to the low heat and stir the mixture until all the sugar has dissolved.

7. Bring to the boil and boil vigorously for 10 minutes then test for setting.

8. Allow the jam to cool for 15 minutes then remove the kernels with a long-handled spoon, taking care as the jam is extremely hot. Stir and ladle it into prepared jars.

9. Label and date the jars when cool.

Variation
To make a spicy-flavoured jam add ½ teaspoon allspice and a pinch of freshly grated nutmeg to the fruit as it is cooking, before adding the sugar.

Storage
This should keep for up to 6 months unopened.

Peach Melba Jam

This is a wonderful combination of peaches and raspberries. Use a sachet of pectin if you prefer a firmer setting jam.

MAKES ABOUT 6 X 500G JARS

1kg firm but ripe peaches
Juice of 2 lemons
250ml water
1kg raspberries
1.5kg sugar
1 x 13g sachet pectin (optional)

1. Cut the peaches in half and remove the stones. For a more concentrated peach flavour remove 2 or 3 of the kernels and add them to the pan with the fruit (see the recipe for Peach Jam above for full details).

2. Put the peaches and any juice in the pan with the water and lemon juice. Simmer for 10 minutes then add the raspberries and continue to simmer until the raspberries just begin to fall or pulp and release their juice. This should only take another few minutes.

3. Add the sugar and pectin (if using) to the fruit over a low heat. Stir constantly until it has all dissolved.

4. Bring to the boil and boil vigorously for 4 minutes then test for setting.

5. Allow to cool, then stir and ladle into sterile jars.

6. Label and date the jars when cool.

Storage
This jam should keep for up to 6 months unopened.

Pear Jam

MAKES ABOUT 5 X 500G JARS

2kg pears
750ml water
Zest and juice of 3 lemons
1.25kg sugar

1. Place the water, lemon zest and juice in the pan. Peel and core the pears and cut into small pieces. Add to the lemon water as you prepare each piece of fruit and stir in thoroughly as this will stop the fruit from discolouring.

2. Bring to a simmer; do not boil as this impairs the flavour of the jam. Continue simmering for about 8 minutes or until the pears are just tender.

3. Stir in the sugar over a low heat and continue stirring until all the sugar has dissolved.

4. Bring the mixture to the boil and boil vigorously for 10 minutes then test for setting.

5. Allow the jam to cool for 5 minutes then stir and ladle it into prepared jars.

6. Label and date the jars when cool.

Storage
This should keep for up to 6 months unopened.

Plum Jam

This recipe uses Victoria plums, but use whatever plums you have. Freshly picked, just ripe or slightly under-ripe fruit give the best flavour and set for this jam.

MAKES ABOUT 10 X 500G JARS

3kg Victoria plums
560ml water
3kg sugar

1. Wash the fruit. Halve and stone the plums or leave the stones attached to the fruit and they will float to the top during cooking. They can then be skimmed away. If you are removing them add a few kernels to the plums as they are cooking, to give extra flavour. If you prefer smaller pieces of fruit in the jam then cut the plums into quarters.

2. Put the fruit and the water in the pan and the kernels if you are using them. Simmer for about 20–25 minutes or until the fruit is beginning to fall or pulp. Remove the kernels with a long-handled spoon.

3. Stir in the sugar and continue to stir until all the sugar has dissolved.

4. Bring the mixture to the boil then boil vigorously for about 10 minutes and test for setting.

5. Allow the jam to cool for 15 minutes then stir and ladle it into prepared jars.

6. Label and date the jars when cool.

Quince Jam

Quinces are very firm, almost woody fruits that look like pears. They are a late-autumn gift for making jams and jellies. They do take a long time to soften so I find it's best to grate them first. Quinces are ready to be used for jam-making when they smell fragrant.

MAKES ABOUT 6 X 500G JARS

2kg quinces
1.5 litres water
Zest and juice of 2 large or 3 small lemons
2kg sugar

1. Put the water, lemon zest and juice in the pan.

2. Cut the fruit in half and remove the core. Grate each of the fruits and place in the pan with the water and lemon. Stir well.

3. Bring to the boil and then simmer for about 10 minutes.

4. Stir in the sugar and continue to stir over a low heat until all the sugar has dissolved.

5. Bring the mixture to the boil and continue to boil for about 30 minutes then test for setting.

6. Allow to cool for 5 minutes then ladle the jam into prepared jars.

7. Label and date the jars when cool.

Soft-set Raspberry Jam

I have two methods for making raspberry jam. This one, which is simple and fresh-flavoured, has a softer set, while the following recipe uses pectin for a firmer set.

MAKES ABOUT 6 X 500G JARS

2kg raspberries
Juice of 1 lemon
2kg sugar

1. Put the raspberries in a pan with the lemon juice and heat to simmering. Cook for about 4 minutes until the juices begin to run.

2. Turn the heat down low and stir in the sugar. Continue to stir until all the sugar has dissolved.

3. Bring the mixture to the boil and continue to boil for about 5 minutes then test for setting.

4. Allow the jam to cool for 5 minutes, stir and ladle it into prepared jars.

5. Label and date the jars when cool.

Firm-set Raspberry Jam

2kg raspberries
Juice of 1 lemon
1.75kg sugar
1 x 13g sachet pectin

1. Put the raspberries and lemon juice in a pan and simmer the fruit until the juices begin to run.

2. Add the sugar and pectin and stir over a low heat until the sugar has dissolved.

3. Bring the mixture rapidly to the boil and boil for 4 minutes. Test for setting.

4. Allow the jam to cool for 5 minutes then stir and ladle into prepared jars.

5. Label and date the jars when cool.

Storage
This should keep for up to 9 months unopened.

Rhubarb Jam

1.5kg rhubarb
Juice of 2 lemons
600ml water
1.5kg sugar
1 x 13g sachet pectin

1. Wash, trim and cut the rhubarb into 1cm pieces and place in a pan with the lemon juice and water.

2. Bring to the boil then simmer for 15–20 minutes or until the rhubarb is tender.

3. Add the sugar and pectin and stir until all the sugar has dissolved.

4. Bring the mixture to the boil and boil for 5–6 minutes then test for setting.

5. Allow the jam to cool for 10 minutes then stir and ladle into prepared jars.

6. Label and date the jars when cool.

Variation
Add about 15g chopped fresh ginger to the jam as it is boiling.

Rhubarb and Orange Jam

MAKES ABOUT 6 X 500G JARS

1.5kg rhubarb
2 large oranges
300ml water
1kg sugar

1. Wash and trim the rhubarb and cut into 1cm pieces.

2. Cut the oranges in half and juice them. Scoop out as much of the flesh as you can. Cut half of one of the orange half skins into very small thin pieces. This can be done in a food processor.

3. Put the rhubarb and orange juice, flesh and peel in a pan with the water.

4. Simmer for about 15–20 minutes or until the rhubarb and peel are tender.

5. Add the sugar and stir until it has all dissolved.

6. Bring the mixture to the boil and continue to boil for 20 minutes then test for setting.

7. Allow the jam to cool for 10 minutes then stir and ladle into prepared jars.

8. Label and date the jars when cool.

Storage
This should keep for up to 9 months unopened.

Smooth Strawberry Jam

In this recipe the fruit is crushed to give a smoother-textured jam.

MAKES ABOUT 7 X 500G JARS

2kg strawberries
Juice of 2 lemons
2kg sugar
2 x 13g sachets pectin

1. Place the fruit in a pan and add the lemon juice. Heat to simmering and cook for 3–4 minutes. As the strawberries cook, use a potato masher to crush most of them.

2. Lower the heat and add the sugar and pectin, stirring constantly until the sugar has dissolved.

3. Bring to the boil and, as soon as the mixture is boiling fully, set the timer and allow it to boil vigorously for 4 minutes.

4. Remove from the heat. Test for setting. If the jam isn't ready, boil for 1 more minute and continue like this until a setting point is reached.

5. Allow the jam to cool for 10 minutes then ladle it into prepared jars.

6. Label and date the jars when cool.

Whole Strawberry Jam

For this recipe whole, uncrushed strawberries are used.
I think this gives the fullest strawberry flavour.

MAKES ABOUT 7 X 500G JARS

2kg strawberries, small and fairly even-sized
1.75kg sugar
Juice of 2 lemons
2 x 13g sachets pectin

1. Wash the fruit and place in a pan. Sprinkle over the sugar, cover and leave overnight.

2. The next day, put the pan over a low heat and add the lemon juice. Stir gently without breaking up the strawberries.

3. Sprinkle in the pectin and bring to the boil as quickly as you can. Once the mixture is boiling vigorously, set the timer for exactly 4 minutes and then test for setting as for Smooth Strawberry Jam at step 4.

4. Allow the mixture to cool for 10 minutes then stir gently and ladle into prepared jars.

5. Label and date the jars when cool.

Storage
Both versions of this jam should keep for up to 9 months.

Strawberry and Apple Jam

1kg cooking apples
1kg strawberries
150ml water
Juice of 2 lemons
2kg sugar

1. Place the water and lemon juice in a pan.

2. Peel the apples very thinly and core and chop them. Add each one to the water and lemon juice as you prepare it, to prevent them discolouring.

3. Simmer the apples for 10 minutes.

4. Add the strawberries and simmer for about 5 minutes more until the juice begins to run from the strawberries.

5. Add the sugar and stir gently over a low heat until the sugar has dissolved.

6. Bring the mixture to the boil and boil vigorously for 8 minutes then test for setting. The length of boiling time will depend on how much pectin there is in the apples. Remove the mixture from the heat every time you test for setting.

7. Allow the jam to cool for 10 minutes then stir and ladle it into prepared jars.

8. Label and date the jars when cool.

Summer Fruit Jam

This can be made using a mixture of strawberries, raspberries, cherries, blackcurrants and red and white currants, all in varying quantities as long as the overall weight of fruit is 2kg. If more than half the weight is made up of blackcurrants no pectin is needed; if they make up less than a quarter of the weight you will require a pectin sachet.

MAKES ABOUT 7 X 500G JARS

2kg summer fruits
Juice of 2 lemons
150ml water
2kg sugar
1 x 13g sachet of pectin if you are using few blackcurrants

1. Wash and prepare the fruit, remembering to remove the cherry stones if you don't want them in your jam.

2. Place the fruit, water and lemon juice in the pan and simmer for about 5 minutes until the juices start to run.

3. Add the sugar and pectin if you are using it and stir over a low heat until the sugar has dissolved.

4. Bring the mixture to the boil and boil vigorously for 4 minutes if you are using pectin then test for setting. If you are not using pectin test for setting point after about 8 minutes.

5. Allow the jam to cool for 15 minutes then stir and ladle it into prepared jars.

6. Label and date the jars when cool.

Tropical Fruit Jam

I like to make this for summer cakes and tarts. It's fun to make and smells wonderful as it is cooking.

MAKES ABOUT 6 X 500G JARS

1kg kiwi fruits, thinly peeled and chopped
Flesh of 3 passion fruits
500g fresh pineapple, chopped
500g mango flesh, chopped
Zest and juice of 2 limes
100ml water
1.75kg sugar
1 x 13g sachet pectin
25g desiccated coconut

1. Put all the fruit, lime zest and juice and the water in a pan and heat to simmering for about 5 minutes.

2. Remove from the heat and stir in the sugar and pectin. Stir over a low heat until all the sugar has dissolved.

3. Bring quickly to the boil and boil continuously for 5 minutes then test for setting.

4. Stir in the coconut and allow the jam to cool for 10 minutes then stir and ladle it into prepared jars.

5. Label and date the jars when cool.

Storage
This will keep for up to 6 months unopened.

Using Frozen Fruit for Jam-making

Jam made from frozen fruits is very successful. It is speedier to make than jam made with fresh fruit as it only needs heating up rather than cooking. The fruit must be totally defrosted before you prepare the jam. You can use home-frozen or shop-bought frozen fruit.

Fruit mixes found in the freezer sections of supermarkets make unusual and delicious combinations. They often come in 500g packs of summer fruit, black forest and autumn fruit mixes. The pectin content of fruit diminishes when it is frozen so, if you want a firmer setting jam, you will need to add pectin.

With frozen strawberries, raspberries and blackberries use an equal amount of sugar to fruit for a firmer setting jam or 80g sugar per 100g fruit for a less sweet and softer set. With these three fruits always add the juice of 1 lemon per kilo of fruit. Again use 1 pectin sachet per kilo of fruit if you require a firmer set.

Frozen Fruit Mixture Jam

This is a simple basic recipe that you can use with any of the
various mixes available.

MAKES ABOUT 3 X 500G JARS

2 x 500g bags of frozen fruit, defrosted
Juice of 1 lemon
900g sugar
1 x 13g sachet pectin, if you require a firmer set

1. Put the sugar in a dish in a low oven heated to 140°C/gas mark 1
for 8 minutes.

2. Put the fruit in a large preserving pan with the lemon juice and
bring to simmering.

3. Remove from the heat and stir in the warmed sugar. Stir in the
pectin if you are using it.

4. Stir the mixture over a very low heat until the sugar dissolves.

5. Bring to the boil and boil for 5 minutes then test for setting point.
Don't overboil as this will impair the fruit flavour.

6. Allow the jam to stand for 10 minutes then stir to distribute the
fruit and ladle into prepared jars.

7. Label and date the jars when cool.

Using Dried Fruit for Jam-making

Dried Apricot Jam

MAKES ABOUT 3 X 500G JARS

1kg dried apricots, chopped as finely as you wish
Water
Juice of 2 lemons
2kg sugar

1. Put the apricots in a bowl and pour over sufficient water to cover the fruit with 3cm of water to spare to allow for the apricots swelling. Leave overnight or for at least 14 hours.

2. Put the fruit and the soaking liquid in a preserving pan with the lemon juice and bring to the boil. Reduce the heat as soon as the liquid is boiling and simmer for 25–30 minutes until the apricots are tender.

3. Remove the pan from the heat and stir in the sugar. Return to the low heat and stir until all the sugar has dissolved.

4. Bring the mixture back to the boil and boil vigorously for 5 minutes then test for setting.

5. When the jam is ready, allow it to stand for 5 minutes then stir and ladle into prepared jars. Label and date the jars when cool.

Variations
Add 80g flaked almonds and ½ to 1 teaspoon almond extract to the jam when it is standing at step 5 and stir well to distribute the almonds and flavouring.

Dried Apricot and Date Jam – use 500g each of apricots and pitted dates, chop them to your required size and soak them overnight in orange or pineapple juice. For a smooth jam, after soaking put the fruit in a food processor and process until it is puréed. This will need about 5 minutes' boiling time to cook before you add the sugar, then continue as step 3 of the **Dried Apricot Jam** recipe.

5. *Making Marmalades*

Marmalade is really just citrus fruit jam. The whole fruit is usually used in its preparation – pips, pith and all. This is because the pith and pips contain pectin which enables the marmalade to produce a good set. The pips are put in a muslin bag during the fruit cooking and lifted out before the sugar is added. Most of the pith will melt into the mixture during the cooking of the fruit, but some citrus fruits, such as lemons and grapefruit, can contain a lot of pith and you may need to trim some of it off.

Points to remember when making marmalade

- Some citrus fruit has a coating on it to preserve it, so wash all fruit in tepid, slightly soapy water and scrub gently with a clean sponge. You can buy uncoated fruit, but you should still wash it well.

- Make your marmalade as soon as you can after purchasing the fruit, to ensure freshness and flavour.

- Because it's difficult to give an accurate weight to citrus fruits, an average weight is given in the recipes. It won't matter if the actual weight of your fruit varies by 50–60g. With grapefruit which are large, you may need to use half of one to get the weight.

- Prepare your fruit over a dish or bowl to catch all the drips of precious juice.

- The fruit may be cooked in a pressure cooker to speed up the cooking time, which is often much longer for citrus fruit. Follow the manufacturer's instructions for timings.

- If you need to use a muslin bag to hold bits and pieces of fruit, use tongs to lift it out of the hot mixture and squeeze out as much of the liquid as possible. It will look slimy and gel-like; this is the pectin that will help set the marmalade.

- When the marmalade is cooking it often produces a scum on the surface. This can be dispersed by adding about half a teaspoon-size knob of butter and stirring. The scum will disappear.

- As with jams, the setting point of the preserve will depend on the fruit and could be different with different batches of fruit. Citrus fruits generally take longer to set than other fruits; the average time is about 20 minutes. Each recipe will give the approximate time.

The Basic Method

1. Wash the fruit to get rid of debris and any coatings. Some recipes include lemons to add acidity so wash these as well.

2. Cut up the unpeeled fruit to your preferred size. Put the pips and any unused pith in a muslin bag and secure. The fruit can be cut up using a food processor if you prefer very small pieces or smoother marmalade.

3. Put the fruit, muslin bag (if using) and water if stated in the recipe in a preserving or sturdy-based pan. Cook for the allotted time until the pith is soft.

4. Remove from the heat and stir in the sugar. Return the pan to a low heat and stir the mixture until there are no sugar crystals on the back of the spoon.

5. Bring the mixture to the boil and continue to boil for the time stated in the recipe. Test for the setting point. Take a small, cold plate and drop a little of the mixture on to it, leave it to cool for a few seconds and push it with your finger; if it wrinkles and stays put the marmalade is ready. Alternatively, push your finger through it to make a channel; if the marmalade is ready the channel should remain rather than run back together.

6. Leave the marmalade to cool for about 10 minutes, and then stir to distribute the peel. Ladle the marmalade into sterilised jars and seal well immediately.

7. Label and date the jars for future reference.

Clementine, Tangerine or Satsuma Marmalade

MAKES ABOUT 2 X 500G JARS

About 600g clementines, tangerines or satsumas or a combination
1 large lemon
1 litre hot water
500g sugar

1. Juice the lemon and place the juice in a pan. Cut the clementines in half and add them to the lemon juice. Pour over the water and add the lemon skins. Bring to the boil, then turn the heat down to simmering and simmer for 30–40 minutes or until the clementine peel is tender.

2. Lift the lemon skins out with tongs and squeeze well, making sure the liquid goes back into the pan.

3. Lift out the clementines and chop them with a knife and fork as they will be hot, or put them into a food processor and whizz until they are chopped to your taste.

4. Return them to the pan and heat to simmering, then remove the pan from the heat and stir in the sugar. Put the pan back onto a low heat and stir until all the sugar has dissolved.

5. Bring the mixture to the boil and boil for 10 minutes then test for setting (see step 5 in the Basic Method).

6. When the marmalade is ready, allow it to cool for 5 minutes then stir and ladle it into prepared jars.

7. Label and date the jars.

Grapefruit Marmalade

MAKES ABOUT 6 X 500G JARS

1kg grapefruit
1 lemon
2 litres hot water
1.5kg sugar

1. Pare the rind from the grapefruit and discard any very large pieces of pith. Cut the rind very finely into shreds of your preferred size and place them in a pan. Chop the fruit into small pieces and add the flesh and all the juice to the pan with the shreds of peel.

2. Put any pips in a muslin bag and add them to the pan.

3. Cut the lemon into quarters and place them in the pan with the grapefruit.

4. Pour over the water and simmer the fruit gently for at least 2 hours until the peel is very soft. Squeeze the lemon quarters with tongs and remove from the pan. These can now be discarded.

5. Remove from the heat and stir in the sugar. Continue to stir until it has dissolved.

6. Bring the mixture to the boil and continue to boil vigorously for 20 minutes then test for setting point (see step 5 in the Basic Method).

7. When the marmalade is ready, leave it to cool for 15 minutes then stir, ladle into prepared jars and seal well.

8. Label and date the jars.

Lemon Marmalade

Here are two recipes for this tangy preserve. See which you find the easiest. Use unwaxed lemons in both recipes, if you can get them; if not, wash and scrub the skins well with warm soapy water, then rinse. Be careful not to scuff the skin as this allows the zest to escape.

MAKES ABOUT 3 X 500G JARS

650–750g lemons
1.8 litres hot water
1.5kg sugar

Method 1

1. Put the whole lemons in the pan with the water, cover and bring quickly to the boil. Then simmer partially covered for 2–2½ hours. Each lemon should be very soft.

2. Remove the fruit from the pan and place in a dish or bowl. Cool until they are easy to handle. Cut the lemons in half and scoop out the insides, putting the flesh and juice into the pan with the other liquid.

3. Bring this to the boil and boil vigorously for 10 minutes. Then strain into another pan. Press the pulp to get as much of the liquid as possible into the pan.

4. Cut the peel into very thin strips and place in the pan. Bring back to the boil and remove from the heat.

5. Stir in the sugar and continue to stir until all the sugar has dissolved.

68

6. Return the pan to the heat, bring the mixture to the boil and boil for at least 10 minutes then test for setting point (see step 5 in the Basic Method).

7. If necessary, add a small knob of butter to distribute any scum from the top.

8. When setting point is reached, allow the marmalade to stand for 5 minutes then stir and ladle into prepared jars.

9. Label and date the jars.

Method 2
1. Peel the rind from the fruit, paring only the zesty part and leaving as much of the pith on the fruit as you can. Cut the peel into very fine shreds.

2. Put the peel in the pan and cut the rest of the lemons in half and juice them. Add the juice to the pan with the peel.

3. Chop up the rest of the flesh into small pieces, discarding any large pieces of pith; the rest will dissolve into the marmalade and help setting. Put the pips in a muslin bag. Put everything together in the pan and add the water.

4. Bring to the boil then simmer, uncovered, for 2 hours or until the peel is tender.

5. Remove from the heat and use tongs to remove the pips bag, squeezing well as you do so.

6. Stir in the sugar and continue to stir until it has all dissolved.

7. Bring the mixture to the boil and boil vigorously for 15 minutes, adding a knob of butter to disperse any scum if necessary, then test for setting point (see step 5 in the Basic Method).

8. When the marmalade is ready, allow it to stand for 5 minutes then stir and ladle into prepared jars.

9. Label and date the jars.

Variation
Whichever method you choose for this recipe, you can vary it by using limes or a combination of lemons and limes.

Orange Marmalade

This recipe uses any type of oranges you may have in your fruit
bowl. The flavour isn't as tangy and orangey, nor is the marmalade
as firm in its set, as if you had used Seville oranges, but this makes
a very good alternative for the times when Sevilles are not available.
It's an easy recipe, one for people who like a chunky marmalade.
I use unrefined golden caster sugar for even easier preparation; it
dissolves much faster and adds a wonderful flavour to the
marmalade.

MAKES ABOUT 5 X 500G JARS

2kg oranges
3 lemons
2 litres water
2kg sugar

1. Wash the skin of the fruit well and quarter the unpeeled oranges.
Remove the pips and put aside. Put the fruit and any juice in a pan.

2. Cut the lemons in half and remove the pips. Squeeze out the juice
and pour over the oranges. Put the skins in the pan and pour over the
water. Put the orange and lemon pips in a muslin bag and add this to
the pan as well.

3. Bring to the boil and then simmer for 2–2½ hours. The orange peel
should be very tender.

4. Lift the lemon skins out with tongs, squeeze and then discard them.

5. Lift the orange peel out and place in a bowl. When it has cooled chop it into pieces of a size to suit your taste. If you like the peel chopped very finely, put it in a food processor until it is the size you require. Return this to the pan.

6. Bring the mixture to the boil and then remove from the heat. Use tongs to lift out the pips bag and again squeeze it to release the liquid.

7. Stir in the sugar and replace the pan on a low heat. Stir until all the sugar has dissolved.

8. Bring the marmalade to the boil and boil vigorously for 20 minutes then test for setting (see step 5 in the Basic Method).

9. Allow to cool for about 10 minutes and then stir and ladle into prepared jars.

10. Label and date the jars.

Quick Orange Marmalade

If you have a microwave you can make two small jars of marmalade
very quickly and easily. I actually find this is best made with the
thin-skinned smaller oranges. You will need a microwaveable bowl
large enough to hold the marmalade as it boils up so that it won't
boil over. I find the bowl needs to be large enough to hold at least
twice the quantity of marmalade mixture.

About 300g oranges
1 large lemon
500ml boiling water
500g sugar

1. Juice the lemon and remove the pips. Put the pips in a muslin bag.

2. Slice the oranges into very thin slices and add the pips to the
muslin bag. Put the oranges, lemon skins and lemon juice in a
microwaveable bowl and cover with 300ml of boiling water. Cover
and leave to steep for 1 hour.

3. Add the remaining 200ml of boiling water and cook on high in the
microwave for 20–25 minutes until the peel is very soft. Remove the
lemon shells and muslin bag with tongs and squeeze out well.

4. Stir in the sugar, making sure it has dissolved.

5. Put the bowl back in the microwave and cook the mixture on high
for 10 minutes and stir. Then cook for a further 10 minutes and
check for setting (see step 5 in the Basic Method).

6. When the marmalade is ready, allow it to stand for 10 minutes then
stir and ladle into prepared jars. Label and date the jars.

Seville Orange Marmalade

January is the time to make your Seville orange marmalade. These oranges make the best marmalade because they are very bitter and, when combined with sugar, their tangy orange flavour is still strong. However, they do have a very short season in this country.

MAKES ABOUT 8–9 X 450G JARS

1.5kg Seville oranges
2.5 litres water
Juice of 2 lemons
2.25kg sugar

1. Wash the fruit, cut in half and squeeze out the juice. Put the juice in a pan, taking care not to waste any of it. Place all the pips in a dish ready to be tied in a muslin bag or square.

2. Scoop out all the pith and flesh from the oranges and put it in the pan. Most of the pith will dissolve in cooking and help the marmalade set, but if there are any very thick bits, cut them away and put them with the pips.

3. Cut the peel into thin strips to suit your taste and put it in the pan with the pith and flesh.

4. Add the water. Put the pips and discarded bits of pith into a muslin bag and tie securely. Add this to the pan also.

5. Bring the mixture to the boil, then turn down the heat and simmer for 2 hours until the peel is very soft. Remove the pips bag with tongs and squeeze out all the juice. You will see that it is quite slimy; this is the pectin being extracted.

6. Remove the pan from the heat and stir in the lemon juice and the sugar.

7. Return the pan to a low heat and stir until all the sugar has dissolved.

8. Bring the marmalade to the boil and boil for 10 minutes, then test for the setting point (see step 5 in the Basic Method).

9. When the marmalade is ready, leave to cool for 10 minutes, stir to distribute the peel evenly and then ladle into prepared jars.

10. Label and date the jars.

Old English Marmalade

MAKES ABOUT 8 X 450G JARS

1.5kg Seville oranges
1kg white sugar
1.25kg soft dark brown sugar
1 tbsp dark treacle
2.5 litres water

1. Follow steps 1–7 of the recipe for Seville Orange Marmalade.

2. When all the sugar has dissolved stir in the treacle.

3. Continue with steps 8 and 9 of the recipe.

6. Making Jellies

This form of preserving is much more time-consuming than jam-making. Only the fruit juice is used in the final boiling, but this produces a clear, jewel-like jelly that is great for those who don't like bits in their jam. Jellies are ideal for glazing fruit tarts and adding to both sweet and savoury sauces. Use them with ice creams and similar desserts.

Jelly-making is also good for fruit that contains a lot of pips, such as raspberries, blackberries, rowan berries and sloes. All jellies will keep for up to 9 months unopened. Once opened, refrigerate and use within 4 weeks.

Equipment for jelly-making
The equipment you will need is the same as for jam-making, plus the following:

A 2-litre measuring jug

A straining bag – it is easiest to use a specially made nylon jelly bag that comes with its own stand. But you can use a large piece of strong muslin or a muslin bag. This can be attached to an upturned stool or suspended on a strong hook. It must be secure as it takes 2–10 hours to strain the juice depending on the type and quantity of fruit used.

A large bowl to catch all the juice – the bigger the better. Make sure it will hold the juice as it is frustrating having to change bowls or watch the juice spill over the top.

Store your jellies in smaller jars than you would use for jam, as you tend to use less of this preserve and the jelly will obviously keep better in unopened jars.

Fruits suitable for jelly-making

Most fruits can be made into jellies, but those with a higher pectin content give a better result. You can always add apples to help with the set. Adding pectin is tricky as it is difficult to gauge the amount for different fruits. However, for the raspberry jelly using pectin is the best way to be sure of a set. Ideal fruits for jelly-making are:

- citrus fruit;
- cooking apples;
- crab apples;
- cranberries;
- blackcurrants;
- damsons;
- blackberries (early-picked fruits are best as they contain more pectin than the later ones);
- gooseberries;
- quinces;
- redcurrants;
- rosehips;
- rowan berries.

Points to remember when making jellies

Do not overcook the fruit or cook at a high temperature as this will spoil the final flavour of the jelly.

Never squeeze the straining bag if you want a clear jelly as more than just the juice will be pushed through. This will not affect the flavour, however, only the look of the jelly.

When boiling the juice and sugar, do this at a gentle boil, not a vigorous one, as with jam-making. Again, too vigorous boiling will spoil the flavour of the finished jelly.

The Basic Method

1. Wash the fruit well, discarding any mouldy or very badly damaged fruits. There is no need to discard bits of stalk as these will be trapped during straining.

2. Place the fruit in a preserving pan and just cover with water. Some fruits, such as blackcurrants and quinces, may require a little more water. Stir in the lemon juice at this point if it is listed in the recipe. Bring the mixture slowly to the boil, then simmer gently until the fruit is tender. Each fruit will require a different cooking time, but it must be tender or the juice won't be easily extracted during straining.

3. To strain the cooked fruit, arrange the jelly bag or muslin securely on the stand (or whatever you are using) and place a large bowl underneath. Ladle the cooked fruit into the bag and leave to strain. This will take between 2 and 10 hours depending on the amount you are making and the type of fruit used. When it is ready the pulp should look dry and the juice will have stopped dripping through.

4. Measure the amount of juice – this must be done as it is the only indicator of how much sugar to use. The amount of juice will depend on each batch of fruit, so it must be done each time. Use a large ladle to transfer the juice into the measuring jug rather than pouring it in from the bowl.

5. For every 100ml of juice add 90g sugar. This is the easiest way to measure the sugar and gives the best setting results. For a less sweet flavour and less firm set, use 75–80g sugar per 100ml of juice. Use white granulated sugar as this gives the clearest finish and best flavour to the jelly. To help the sugar dissolve quickly, place it in an ovenproof dish or shallow roasting pan and heat for 10 minutes at 140°C/gas mark 1. You can warm your sterile jars at the same time. If you stand them on a baking sheet it is easier to lift them in and out

of the oven. Turn off the heat when you have removed the sugar. The jars can be removed just before you need to fill them.

6. Pour the juice back into the pan and bring slowly to a fast simmer, turn down the heat and add the sugar. Stir well over a very low heat until all the sugar has dissolved. Check the back of the spoon for sugar crystals to make sure.

7. Bring the mixture to the boil and boil gently rather than too vigorously; it will still set. Check for setting point after 8 minutes as you would with jam. Take a cold plate or saucer and drop a small amount of the mixture onto it. Allow it to cool then push it with your finger; if it wrinkles and remains in place it is ready. If it is not ready, boil for 2 more minutes. While they are boiling, some fruits develop a scum on the top; this can be removed with a large flattish spoon or a fish slice. Skim the surface under the scum and lift it away.

8. Use a preserving funnel to help with potting the jelly. Ladle the jelly carefully into the prepared jars. Do this slowly; if it is done quickly air bubbles can appear in your jelly, spoiling both the look and the eventual quality of your jelly. Seal with the lids immediately, so that the least amount of air enters the jars. This ensures the jelly will keep fresh for the longest period.

9. Label the jars. This is a very important step in all preserving, but especially with jellies as the only clue you have to the contents is the colour. Label the jars clearly with the type of jelly and the date it was made.

A note about the yield
This varies from fruit to fruit and even from batch to batch, so a guide is given with each fruit; this will be very approximate and over-estimated, but gives you an idea of how many jars to sterilise. It is better to have too many than have to fiddle about quickly trying to sterilise another jar.

Apple Jelly

MAKES ABOUT 5 X 450G JARS

2.5kg cooking apples
Juice of 1 lemon
Water to just cover

1. Cut the apples into small chunks. There is no need to peel or core the fruit.

2. Follow the Basic Method above.

Blackberry Jelly

MAKES ABOUT 4 X 450G JARS

2.5kg blackberries
Juice of 2 lemons
Water to just cover

Use early-picked blackberries if you can, as these contain the most pectin. Otherwise combine with cooking apples and follow the recipe for Blackberry and Apple Jelly below.

1. Make sure the fruit is washed and leave whole to cook.

2. Follow the Basic Method above.

Blackberry and Apple Jelly

2kg blackberries
1kg cooking apples
Juice of 2 lemons
Water to just cover

1. Cut the apples into small chunks. There is no need to peel or core the fruit. You need only wash the blackberries and leave them whole to cook.

2. Follow the Basic Method above.

Blackcurrant Jelly

THE YIELD IS HIGHER THAN WITH OTHER FRUITS,
SO THIS COULD MAKE UP TO 6 X 450G JARS

2kg blackcurrants
Water to cover with 2cm to spare

1. There is no need to top and tail the fruit; just wash thoroughly. Blackcurrants take more water than most other fruits so make sure there is 2cm of water above the fruit.

2. Follow the Basic Method above. The fruit will take about 30 minutes or longer to become tender.

Crab Apple Jelly

MAKES ABOUT 4 X 450G JARS

2.5kg crab apples
Juice of 1 lemon
Water to just cover

1. Cut the fruit into small chunks and cook until tender. Don't try to mash down the apples as the juice becomes very difficult to extract from the pulp.

2. Follow the Basic Method above.

Cranberry Jelly

MAKES ABOUT 2 X 450G JARS

1kg cranberries
Apple juice to just cover

1. Simply wash the fruit and get rid of any very soft berries. Cook the cranberries gently for at least 30 minutes in the apple juice.

2. Follow the Basic Method above. Use 80g sugar to every 100ml of juice for this recipe.

Damson Jelly

This produces the tastiest jelly of all, in my opinion. The colour is an amazing deep, bluey purple. It's well worth growing a damson tree simply to have the fruit for making jams and jellies.

MAKES ABOUT 4 X 450G JARS

2kg damsons
Juice of 2 lemons
Water to cover with 2cm to spare

1. Halve the damsons to speed up cooking time. Cook with the stones; this adds flavour and pectin to the jelly.

2. Follow the Basic Method above. Damson jelly may take up to 40 minutes to give a set, so don't be alarmed if it seems to be taking ages.

Gooseberry Jelly

This jelly is an amazing orangey pink colour, quite different from what you would expect.

MAKES ABOUT 4 X 450G JARS

2.5kg gooseberries
Water to just cover fruit

1. Simply wash and cook the fruit.

2. Follow the Basic Method above.

Variation
To make a delicious Gooseberry and Elderflower Jelly, simply add 2–4 elderflower heads to the gooseberries as they are cooking. The more flower heads you use the more intense the flavour of the jelly.

Lemon Jelly

The method for citrus fruits is different from that for other, non-citrus fruit. Use unwaxed lemons for this recipe if you can get them. If not, wash and scrub the skins gently in warm, slightly soapy water and rinse well.

MAKES ABOUT 4 X 450G JARS

2kg unwaxed lemons
Water

1. Peel the lemons and place the rind in a muslin bag.

2. Put the fruit in a bowl and chop into small chunks inside the bowl so that all the juice is retained.

3. Place the muslin bag in the centre of the chopped fruit and pour over sufficient cold water to cover. Allow to steep overnight.

4. The next day transfer everything to a preserving pan, bring to the boil, and simmer gently for about 1½ hours or until the rind is tender.

5. Remove the bag of rind and pour the contents of the pan into the straining bag and allow to strain until the juice stops dripping from the bottom of the bag.

6. Measure the juice and weigh the appropriate amount of sugar. This is 105g sugar to every 100ml of juice. Warm the sugar in the oven for 10 minutes at 140°C/gas mark 1.

7. Put the juice and the bag of rind in the pan and bring to the boil. Remove from the heat and use tongs to remove the bag of rind, gently squeezing the juice and slimy liquid back into the pan.

8. Stir in the sugar and return the pan to a low heat. Stir until all the sugar has dissolved.

9. Bring the mixture to the boil and boil until a setting point is reached.

10. Allow the jelly to cool then ladle into prepared jars and label.

Variation
Orange Jelly can be prepared in the same way.

Grape Jelly

Grapes containing seeds give the best set. If you wish to use
seedless grapes add a cooking apple to the fruit while it is cooking.
Simply peel, core and chop it.

MAKES ABOUT 2 X 450G JARS

1.5kg grapes, any colour you like
Water to just cover

1. Cook the grapes gently until the skins are soft.

2. Follow the Basic Method above.

Raspberry Jelly

MAKES ABOUT 3 X 450G JARS

2kg raspberries
Juice of 1 lemon
650ml water
1 x 13g sachet pectin

1. Put the raspberries in a pan with the lemon juice and water and
simmer until the fruit is soft. This will take about 15 minutes.

2. Follow steps 3 onwards of the Basic Method, allowing 80g sugar
per 100ml juice.

Redcurrant Jelly

MAKES ABOUT 3 X 450G JARS

2kg redcurrants
Water to just cover

1. Wash and pull the fruit from the stems using a fork. Place in a pan, just cover with water and simmer until tender.

2. Follow the Basic Method above, using 90g sugar per 100ml juice.

Rowan Jelly

This is a great accompaniment to cooked meats.

MAKES 500–700G

1.5kg rowan berries
Juice of 1 lemon
Water to cover

1. Remove the berries from any stalks and place them in the pan with the lemon juice and water. Bring to the boil then simmer for 20 minutes or until tender. Use a potato masher to squash the fruit as it cooks to release the juices.

2. Follow the Basic Method above, but don't try testing for a setting point until after the mixture has been boiling for 15 minutes.

Rosehip Jelly

This is a delightful light pinkish jelly, ideal for glazing fruit tarts and the tops of fruit cakes. Rosehips are low in pectin so I find it easier to use jam sugar that contains pectin or add a sachet when adding the sugar. You could also combine the hips with half the amount of crab apples, to help the setting of the jelly.

MAKES 300–400G

1kg rosehips
Juice of ½ lemon
Water

1. Chop the hips roughly and place them in a pan with the lemon juice and enough water to cover with 1cm to spare. Bring to the boil then turn down the heat and simmer for 25–30 minutes or until the hips are tender.

2. Follow the Basic Method above. If you are using crab apples, chop them and cook them with the hips.

Strawberry and Apple Jelly

MAKES ABOUT 3–4 X 450G JARS

2kg strawberries
1kg cooking apples
Water to just cover

1. Hull the strawberries if you wish and chop the apples, unpeeled, into fairly small chunks. Place all the fruit in a pan, just cover with water and simmer until the apples are tender.

2. Follow the Basic Method above.

7. Making Fruit Curds, Cheeses and Butters

These are delicacies of yesteryear, and, though not as popular to make at home today, they are still worth the effort. The butters are particularly good for those with less of a sweet tooth as they contain half the amount of sugar. They were often served with high tea, to spread on slices of bread instead of jams and other preserves, particularly when serving tea to guests. The cheeses and butters were used to fill pies, tarts and cakes.

These are not long-lasting preserves and should be eaten fairly quickly, especially once the jars have been opened, so are best made in small quantities. There is no setting point to worry about in any of the processes.

Curds

Lemon curd is still a very popular cake and tart filling. Many people call this lemon cheese, although traditionally lemon cheese is lemon pulp simmered with sugar to make a thick purée. Lemon curd is made with butter and eggs. Curds are not prepared in the same way as jams and jellies; they are not boiled and the egg content means their shelf life is much shorter. However, they do freeze for up to three months and this doesn't seem to affect the flavour or texture. A popular curd served in Victorian households was made with apricots and is an excellent alternative to lemon curd. It can be used in tarts or as a layer in desserts such as trifles and fruit flans. It uses dried apricots so can be made at any time, so long as you have some in the store cupboard.

Apricot Curd

MAKES 1 X 500G JAR

180g dried apricots
Water to cover the apricots
230g white caster sugar
60g butter
Juice of 1 lemon
2 eggs

1. Put the apricots in a bowl and cover them in warm water. Leave to soak overnight or for at least 12 hours.

2. Put the apricots and any liquor in a pan and simmer, not boil, until tender.

3. Push the fruit through a sieve or place in a blender or food processor and blend to make a purée.

4. Put the apricot purée and the sugar in a double boiler or a bowl that fits over a pan of boiling water. Stir over the heat until the sugar dissolves.

5. Add the butter and lemon juice and stir until the butter melts.

6. Beat the eggs. Remove the apricot mixture from the heat and stir the eggs into the fruit mixture.

7. Replace the bowl over the boiling water and stir until the curd thickens.

8. Pour into a sterile jar or jars.

9. Label and date the jars. It's best to give a 'use by' date of 2 weeks from the date of making, to be safe.

Lemon Curd

This can also be made with oranges.

MAKES ABOUT 2 X 450G JARS

4 large lemons
450g white caster sugar
230g butter
5 eggs

1. Grate the zest off the lemons and place in a heatproof bowl. Squeeze out all the juice and add to the zest. Place the bowl over a pan of boiling water or use a double boiler.

2. Add the sugar and stir until it has all dissolved.

3. Stir in the butter until it melts.

4. In a separate bowl beat the eggs and remove the bowl of lemon mixture from the heat. Stir the eggs into the mixture.

5. Replace the bowl over the boiling water and stir the mixture until the curd thickens.

6. Pour into sterile jars and label and date the jars when cool.

Storage
As this has a higher sugar content than the Apricot Curd it will keep for a month unopened and stored in the fridge. Once open use within 2 weeks. Both curd recipes will freeze for 3 months.

Fruit cheeses
These will keep for about 2 months in a fridge, unopened. The yield isn't high and on average amounts to about half of the total weight of fruit.

Fruit butters
These are best stored in small sterile lidded pots in the fridge and eaten within 4 weeks. The yield is similar to or slightly lower than that of cheese.

Equipment for making fruit cheeses and butters
Besides the obvious pan and jars, the other equipment you will need for making cheeses and butters is a large nylon or plastic sieve and some scales to weigh the pulp.

The Basic Method

1. Prepare the fruit. Wash and discard any of poor quality. Chop larger fruit into small chunks. Leave berries whole. There is no need to peel fruit or cut away cores or little bits of stem as the fruit is sieved in the process.

2. Place the fruit in a pan and add lemon juice if necessary and water as required; the amounts of lemon juice and water will be specified in the individual recipes. Cook the fruit until very tender.

3. Rub the cooked fruit through a nylon or plastic sieve to produce a fine pulp.

4. Weigh the pulp and place in the preserving pan. Some fruit pulps are simmered before adding the sugar; instructions will be given in the individual recipes.

5. Weigh the sugar. For fruit cheese add the same weight of sugar as fruit pulp. For fruit butter add half the weight of the pulp in sugar.

6. Add the sugar to the fruit pulp and stir over a low heat until the sugar dissolves.

7. Simmer for 45 minutes to 1 hour. There should be no free liquid in either of the mixtures when it is ready to pot. It should look firm and hold its shape when a spoonful is lifted up.

8. Spoon into prepared sterile pots and cover immediately.

Fruit cheeses

Apple Cheese

3kg apples (if using dessert apples, add the juice of 1 lemon)
1 litre water
500ml cider or apple juice
Sugar as necessary (see step 5 of the Basic Method)

1. Follow the Basic Method, but simmer the pulp for about 30 minutes before adding the sugar. This will allow most of the liquid to evaporate.

Variation
For Spiced Apple Cheese, add ½ – 1 teaspoon ground cinnamon and a pinch of grated nutmeg to the apple pulp when you add the sugar.

Blackberry and Apple Cheese

1kg blackberries
500g cooking apples
300ml water
Sugar as necessary (see step 5 of the Basic Method)

Follow the Basic Method above.

Blackcurrant Cheese

2kg blackcurrants
2 litres water
Sugar as necessary (see step 5 of the Basic Method)

Follow the Basic Method above, but simmer the pulp for about 30 minutes before adding the sugar.

Damson Cheese

3kg damsons
350ml water
Sugar as necessary (see step 5 of the Basic Method)

Follow the Basic Method above, but simmer the pulp for about 20 minutes before adding the sugar.

Gooseberry Cheese

2kg gooseberries
450ml water
Sugar as necessary (see step 5 of the Basic Method)

Follow the Basic Method above. Leave the fruit whole when cooking.

Plum Cheese

2kg plums
Water if necessary
Sugar as necessary (see step 5 of the Basic Method)

Follow the Basic Method above, but only add 200ml water if most of the plums are very firm and under-ripe. Ripe plums won't need any water adding during cooking, but halving them speeds up the cooking time. Leave the stones in the fruit.

Rhubarb Cheese

2kg rhubarb, cut into 1cm chunks
Juice of 2 lemons
200ml water
Sugar as necessary (see step 5 of the Basic Method)

Follow the Basic Method above.

Fruit butters

For butters follow the recipes and Basic Method above, but add half the weight of the pulp in sugar rather than equal weight.

8. Making Special Preserves

These are preserves for special occasions – to present as gifts,
perhaps, or maybe just because you fancy making something extra
special as a treat for yourself and your family or friends. There are
three mincemeat recipes and a rather unusual Hodgkin, which is
basically fruit preserved in alcohol. The rest are conserves, which
are similar to jams but don't have such a long storage life and are
usually a soft set. However, I'm sure the shelf life of these preserves
won't be a problem as they are so delicious they will be consumed
in no time!

Mincemeat

Christmas just wouldn't be the same without mince pies. Yes, there
are some excellent pots of mincemeat available in the shops, but
making your own is just so easy. You can customise it to your own
taste, adding a little more spice or fewer cherries, for example. The
brandy may be omitted from the first recipe if you prefer, although
the alcohol helps to preserve and flavour the fruit.

Easy Mincemeat

An absolute must to make in late October for use over Christmas.

MAKES ABOUT 5 X 450G JARS

450g Bramley or other cooking apples
1kg mixed dried fruit: raisins, currants and sultanas
110g glacé cherries, halved or whole, whichever you prefer
225g vegetarian suet
280g soft brown sugar
Zest and juice of 1 lemon
½ teaspoon mixed spice
½ teaspoon ground cinnamon
½ teaspoon grated nutmeg
5 tablespoons brandy

1. Core and dice the apples and cook over a low heat until just soft. Leave to cool.

2. Put all the dried fruit, cherries and cooked apples in a large bowl with the suet, sugar, lemon zest and juice and spices. Mix well together.

3. Sprinkle over the brandy and mix thoroughly to ensure everything is well coated in brandy.

4. Pack into sterile jars and seal well.

Storage
Store for at least 4 weeks before using. Use within 5–6 months.

Variations
Add 150g chopped almonds or hazelnuts to the dried fruit.
Add 200g chopped apricots to the dried fruit.

Almond and Amaretto Mincemeat

500g Bramley or other cooking apples
1kg dried mixed fruit
200g candied peel
110g glacé cherries
400g vegetarian suet
400g soft brown sugar
80g flaked or chopped almonds
1 level teaspoon mixed spice
½ teaspoon ground cinnamon
Zest and juice of 2 lemons
4 tablespoons Amaretto
5 tablespoons rum

1. Put the dried fruit, peel, cherries, suet, sugar, almonds and spices in a large bowl and mix together well.

2. Stir in the lemon juice and zest.

3. Sprinkle over the Amaretto and rum and stir in thoroughly so that all the ingredients are well coated. Cover and leave for 2 hours.

4. Core and dice the apples and cook over a low heat until just tender.

5. Allow the apples to cool completely then stir them into the other ingredients.

6. Pack into sterile jars and seal well.

Storage
Leave to mature for 2–4 weeks.

No Suet Mincemeat

This recipe contains no suet, just a little butter. This helps keep it moist and preserves it.

MAKES ABOUT 700G

250g each of raisins, sultanas, currants and cooking apples, finely chopped
250g soft, dark brown sugar
100g glacé cherries
100g candied peel
120g butter, warmed to just melting
Zest and juice of 1 lemon
Zest and juice of ½ orange
½ teaspoon ground cinnamon
½ teaspoon mixed spice
Good pinch of grated nutmeg
100ml cream sherry
100ml brandy

1. Put all the ingredients except for the butter, sherry and brandy together in a large mixing bowl. Mix well together.

2. Pour over the melted butter and stir thoroughly to coat all the ingredients.

3. Stir in the sherry and brandy.

4. Cover and leave overnight to infuse.

5. Stir thoroughly then pack into jars and seal well.

Storage
Allow to mature for 2 weeks before using.

Hodgkin

This amazing preserve is the easiest of all preserves to prepare but does take a long time before it is ready to consume. It is similar to a rumtopf, but originates in Kent and is made with brandy. I find cheaper brandy gives the best flavour to the preserve.

Because you layer the fruit in the order in which it appears throughout the year, this is almost like a fruit calendar. The fruit is preserved in the brandy and the Hodgkin becomes both a drink and a dessert. You begin layering the fruit in early summer and finish when the last fruits of autumn have been picked. So the first layers are strawberries and raspberries and the last apples and pears.

You will need a large open-necked jar with a securely fitting lid. Each layer of fruit is sprinkled with sugar and covered with brandy. The fruit is layered in the jar until it is full. The Hodgkin will be ready to serve by Christmas time. What a celebration of the year's produce!

How to Prepare Hodgkin

You will need 200–250g of each fruit, depending on how large your jar is, and about 2 tablespoons of white granulated sugar to sprinkle over the fruit before pouring over the brandy. I have found it is better not to use blackcurrants and gooseberries in Hodgkin as they overpower all the other fruits both in flavour and colour. However, you could prepare one in the same way using those two fruits.

1. Prepare the fruit as detailed below. You don't have to use all the fruits listed, just the ones you have or prefer. Wash everything well before adding it to the jar.

- Strawberries – hull and halve
- Raspberries – hull
- Cherries – stone if you wish
- Peaches – stone and quarter, or slice thickly
- Apricots – stone and halve

- Redcurrants – top and tail
- Blackberries – hull
- Plums – stone and halve or quarter
- Damsons – stone and halve
- Dessert apples – core and slice thickly
- Pears – core and quarter

2. Make sure the jar is spotlessly clean, even though the alcohol in the brandy will preserve the fruit.

3. After each addition of fruit, sugar and brandy, seal the lid well and store the jar in a cool, dark place.

4. After adding the last layer of fruit, finish with a layer of brandy that covers the fruit by at least 2cm before sealing the lid.

Serving suggestions
The liquor can be drunk and the fruits eaten with cream or whatever you prefer. Try them in a trifle or at the base of crème brûlée.

Conserves

Conserves are not supposed to be firmly set, but are highly flavoured with fruits and other ingredients. Alcohol helps to preserve conserves, but can be omitted.

Black Cherry Conserve

MAKES ABOUT 3 X 450G JARS

1.5kg black cherries
225g redcurrant jelly
1.25kg sugar
Juice of 1 lemon
2–3 tablespoons cherry brandy or kirsch (optional)

1. Pit the cherries in a bowl to catch any juice and put aside.

2. Put the redcurrant jelly in a pan with any cherry juice, the sugar and lemon juice. Stir over a low heat until the sugar has dissolved.

3. Bring the mixture to the boil then add the cherries and simmer vigorously for 10 minutes, stirring occasionally.

4. Remove the pan from the heat and stir in the brandy or kirsch if you are using any.

5. Allow the mixture to cool for 5 minutes then stir and ladle into prepared jars. Label the jars when cool.

Storage
This should keep for up to 3 months in a cool, dark place. Once opened, store in the fridge and consume within 4 weeks.

Peach Conserve

If you want the conserve to have a firmer set, add a 13g sachet of pectin with the sugar and boil for 4 minutes only then check for setting. The brandy may be omitted if you wish.

MAKES ABOUT 3 X 450G JARS

1.5kg peaches, stoned and chopped (peel if you wish)
100g flaked almonds
80g glacé cherries
Zest and juice of 1 lemon
1kg sugar
5 tablespoons brandy (optional)

1. Place the peaches and any juice in a pan with the almonds, cherries and lemon zest and juice. Bring slowly to the boil.

2. Boil for 5 minutes, then lower the heat and stir in the sugar. Stir constantly until all the sugar has dissolved then boil for 10 minutes.

3. Remove the mixture from the heat and stir in the brandy if using.

4. Cool for 5 minutes, stir and ladle into prepared jars.

5. Label the jars when cool.

Storage
Store as for Black Cherry Conserve.

Peach Melba Conserve

This can be served on top of ice cream or in a tart.

MAKES ABOUT 4 X 450G JARS

1kg peaches, stoned and chopped
500g raspberries
Juice of 1 lemon
1kg sugar
2–3 tablespoons peach or raspberry liqueur (optional)

1. Place the fruit in a pan with the lemon juice and any juice from the peaches. Simmer for 5 minutes or until the juices run from the raspberries.

2. Remove from the heat and stir in the sugar. Return the pan to the heat and stir until all the sugar has dissolved.

3. Bring the mixture to the boil and boil for 10 minutes.

4. Remove from the heat and stir in the liqueur if using, then ladle into prepared jars.

5. Label the jars when cool.

Storage
Store as for Black Cherry Conserve.

Plum Conserve

This is delicious at the base of a steamed sponge pudding, served with custard on a cold autumn evening. Omit the rum if you prefer.

MAKES ABOUT 7 X 450G JARS

2kg plums
200g raisins
300ml water
1.5kg sugar
100g chopped almonds
5 tablespoons rum (optional)

1. Cut the plums in half and remove the stones. Put the stones in a pan with the water, bring to the boil then reduce the heat and simmer for 10 minutes. The water will be infused with flavour to add to the conserve.

2. Remove the stones and put the plums and raisins in the water. Bring to the boil then reduce the heat and simmer for 10–15 minutes or until the plums are just tender.

3. Remove from the heat and add the sugar. Place the pan over a low heat and stir until all the sugar has dissolved.

4. Bring the mixture to the boil then simmer for 10 minutes.

5. Stir in the almonds and rum, if using. Leave to stand for 10 minutes then stir and ladle into prepared jars.

6. Label the jars when cool.

Storage
Store as for Black Cherry Conserve.

Raspberry Conserve

MAKES ABOUT 5 X 450G JARS

1.5kg raspberries
1.25kg sugar
3 tablespoons Framboise or raspberry liqueur (optional)

1. Warm the sugar in a heatproof dish in a very low oven, 140°C/gas mark 1, for 10–15 minutes.

2. Meanwhile put the fruit in a pan and heat gently to simmering. Remove from the heat as soon as the juice from the fruit begins to run.

3. Stir in the warm sugar, return the pan to a low heat and stir the mixture until all the sugar has dissolved.

4. Bring to the boil, stirring occasionally but taking care not to break up the raspberries. When the mixture is boiling turn down to a fast simmer and cook for a further 2–3 minutes.

5. Cool the mixture for 5 minutes then stir gently and add the liqueur if using. Ladle into prepared jars and label when cool.

Storage
This should keep for 8 weeks in a cool, dark place.

Strawberry Conserve

Make this in the same way as the Raspberry Conserve with the same amounts of fruit and sugar. If you wish to add a liqueur, add 3 tablespoons of Grand Marnier.

Winter Conserve

This is an excellent substitute for mincemeat and can be used in the same way or as you would jam.

MAKES ABOUT 3 X 450G JARS

450g prunes, the no-soak ones are the best
350g raisins
100g no-soak apricots, chopped
120g mixed nuts, chopped
600ml warm water
5 tablespoons brandy
600g sugar

1. Put the fruit and nuts in a bowl and pour over the water and the brandy. Stir well and cover. Leave overnight.

2. The next day put the soaked mixture in a pan and heat gently. Stir in the sugar and continue to stir until all the sugar has dissolved.

3. Bring the mixture to the boil. Continue to boil for 5 minutes then turn down the heat and simmer for 15–20 minutes or until the liquid has thickened.

4. Allow the mixture to cool for 5 minutes then stir and ladle into prepared jars. Label when cool.

Storage
This will keep for up to 6 months, unopened. Once open keep in the fridge and eat within 4 weeks.

9. Making Pickles

Pickling is still an important way to preserve your harvests. Apart from vinegar, seasonings and spices and in some cases sugar, the only ingredients are the fruit and vegetables. Pickles generally keep well, so, with just a couple of days' preparation, you can have a year's supply of excellent accompaniments to your meals.

Equipment for making pickles

IMPORTANT: never use copper pans to prepare your pickles. Vinegar reacts with copper and spoils the pickles. Copper ions are released into the pickles and can cause poisoning, not to mention wrecking your pan! Instead use **enamel, stainless steel** or **aluminium pans** with nylon or **plastic sieves** or **strainers** and **wooden** or **stainless-steel spoons**.

Some **large bowls** or **deep dishes** are useful as the vegetables need salting prior to pickling.

If you don't want the spices remaining in the vinegar, some **small squares of muslin** or **muslin bags** are good to hold the pickling spices while still infusing the vinegar.

Jars must be airtight, so a secure lid is essential. If the lids are made of metal make sure they are lined with plastic; most jar lids are these days. I find screw-top lids are best for total security against contamination and spoiling of the pickles. Jars with wide necks are the easiest and quickest to fill. As with all preserve jars they must be sterilised before use. You will also need **large lidded jars** for preparing the vinegar.

There are recipes for five main varieties of pickle in this chapter: cold or raw pickles; cooked pickles; sweet vegetable pickles and those that don't use the spiced vinegar; blended pickles like mustard and brown pickle; and fruit pickles.

Four steps to perfect pickles

There are four main steps to pickling: preparing the vinegar: preparing the vegetables or fruit; making the actual preserve; and storing it. This last step is very important as it allows the pickles time to mature, so that the flavours will develop as the seasoned vinegar permeates the ingredients.

Step 1: Prepare the Vinegar

Pickles are usually preserved in spiced vinegars that give the best possible flavour to the preserve. The type of vinegar varies depending on what you are pickling; malt-based brown and distilled white vinegar are the cheapest and most widely used. But always use good-quality vinegar as it must hold the contents for many months. Wine- and cider-based vinegars may also be used but they are much more expensive and have such a delicate flavour that often it is overpowered by the pickles. However, in some delicately flavoured fruit and vegetables they give a very good result.

Spiced vinegars are best left to mature for at least 4 weeks before using, but may be left for up to 8 weeks, so don't worry if you have to delay making your pickles for some reason, this will be fine.

Use whole spices as they give the best flavour and don't cloud the vinegar. You can also buy a ready mix of whole spices if you prefer but the following recipes will give you a variety of flavours. The quantities for all the recipes may be doubled as necessary.

For sweet pickles
1 litre vinegar
280g brown sugar
½ teaspoon salt
4 whole cloves
½ teaspoon mixed allspice berries and white peppercorns
7g piece of cinnamon
5g piece of root ginger

For mild pickles
1 litre vinegar

*½ teaspoon each of cloves, cinnamon bark, mace, allspice berries and
white peppercorns*

For hot pickles
*1 litre vinegar
25g each of allspice and mustard seed
15g each of white peppercorns and whole cloves
½ teaspoon dried crushed chillies*

1. For all sweet pickle recipes, pour the vinegar into a jug and dissolve the sugar by stirring constantly until all the granules have disappeared. Check the back of the spoon to make sure there are no sugar crystals sticking to it.

2. For all types of pickle recipes, pour the vinegar into a storage jar. Put the various spices into the vinegar, either in a muslin bag or, if you prefer, straight into the vinegar.

3. Leave to mature for 6–8 weeks, shaking the jar gently from time to time.

Quick Spiced Vinegar
If you haven't prepared any vinegar but get the chance to make some pickles, try the following recipe. It will be ready in about 2½ hours.

1. Pour sufficient vinegar to cover your pickles into a double boiler, or use a heatproof glass bowl over a pan of cold water.

2. Add the correct quantity of spices for your chosen flavour from the above recipes. Add the spices directly to the vinegar; don't put them in a muslin bag as this will impair the flavour.

3. Bring to the boil, then remove the pan from the heat but keep the vinegar bowl over the hot water, so both the vinegar in the bowl and the water cool down together.

4. Strain if you wish and use for your pickles.

Step 2: Prepare the Fruit and Vegetables

It is of the utmost importance, especially when preparing raw pickles, that only fresh and undamaged fruit and vegetables are used. If any are bruised or damaged this could lead to the whole jar being spoilt. Wash well and peel and chop according to the instructions for each recipe. Whole fruit and vegetables are usually pricked to prevent them shrinking in the vinegar.

Soaking the vegetables in brine

Some vegetables are salted or soaked in brine for a time to kill off bacteria and improve the storage life of the pickles. This also encourages the pickles to remain submerged and not float on the surface of the vinegar.

To make a brine solution
120g coarse salt (table salt clouds pickling vinegar so is best avoided)
1 litre water

1. Stir the salt into the water and use when all the salt has dissolved.

2. To ensure that the vegetables remain submerged in the solution, keep them pressed down with a plate.

3. After brining or salting, rinse the vegetables thoroughly in cold water and drain well.

Step 3: Bottle the Pickles

Cold or raw pickling

1. Pack the vegetables into sterile jars, leaving about 2cm of space at the top of the jar.

2. Pour over the vinegar, covering by at least 1cm. Some pickles require the vinegar to be heated or even brought to the boil before pouring over the vegetables.

3. Screw on the lids immediately and label and date the jars.

Hot pickling

1. Pack the vegetables into hot jars just after cooking and cover by at least 1cm with the vinegar.

2. Seal the jars with the lids while still hot. Label and date when cool.

Fruit pickling

Each recipe will have its own quantity of sugar and method of pickling.

1. The fruit should be packed into the jars in the same way as the vegetables, leaving about 2cm space at the top of the jar.

2. Cover with vinegar syrup by about 1cm.

With all pickles it is impossible to say exactly how much vinegar will be needed to cover each jar of produce, but any left over may be kept and used in bottling other produce.

Step 4: Store the Pickles

Once bottled and sealed, most uncooked pickles should be left to mature for 4–8 weeks to give the best results. Onions should be left for 8 weeks to give the best balance of flavour. However, pickled cabbage can be eaten after just 6 days. Most cooked pickles can be eaten after about 7 days of maturing.

All pickles are best kept in a cool, dark place and consumed within 9 months if unopened. Some, like pickled beetroot, may need to be eaten within 8 weeks. Once opened, refrigerate and use within 3 weeks.

A note about the recipes

The recipes don't include a measure of vinegar as this will vary greatly. So always have at least 1 litre of vinegar ready unless more is indicated in the recipe. Neither is it possible to give the amounts each recipe makes as these also vary greatly.

Uncooked pickle recipes

Pickled Cabbage

Red or white cabbage may be used in this recipe.

1 large cabbage
Coarse salt
Spiced vinegar (see page 111)

1. Choose a firm, fresh cabbage and remove all the outer loose leaves and any that are damaged.

2. Shred the cabbage as finely as you prefer. The tough inner core can be used to make soups or else discarded.

3. Put a layer of cabbage in a large bowl and cover with a layer of salt. Continue to layer the cabbage with salt in this way, finishing with a layer of salt. Leave for 24 hours.

4. Drain away the salty liquor and rinse the cabbage in cold water.

5. Pack into sterile jars and cover with the spiced vinegar.

6. Seal well and label and date the jars.

Storage
This can be eaten after 6 days. If unopened, red cabbage will keep for 3 months, white cabbage for 2 months. Once opened, refrigerate and use within 4 weeks.

Pickled Cauliflower

Pickled cauliflower tastes best if the vinegar is slightly sweet. Add 2 teaspoons of white granulated sugar per 500ml of vinegar a few days before it is needed.

3 cauliflower heads
Spiced vinegar (see page 111)
Sugar (see above)

For the brine
300g coarse salt
1 litre water

1. Wash the cauliflower heads well and cut into small florets.

2. Soak in a brine solution for 24 hours (see page 113).

3. Rinse well, drain and pat dry with a cloth.

4. Pack into sterile jars and cover with the vinegar. Seal immediately.

Storage
This is best left for 1 month before consuming and will keep for 6 months unopened.

Pickled Cucumbers

3 medium cucumbers
Spiced vinegar (see page 111)
Salt

1. Wash and dry the cucumbers and chop into thick slices. Layer the slices in a dish and salt each layer liberally. Leave for 24 hours.

2. Just before you need it, heat the spiced vinegar until it's just simmering.

3. Drain the cucumber liquid and rinse off the salt.

4. Pack the cucumber into sterile jars and pour over the hot vinegar. Seal well immediately.

Storage
This will be ready to eat after 5 days and will keep for up to 6 months unopened.

Pickled Gherkins

1kg gherkins
Spiced vinegar (see page 111)

For the brine solution
300g coarse salt
1 litre water

1. Wash the gherkins and prick all over before soaking in brine for 3 days (see page 113).

2. Drain and rinse in hot water.

3. Heat the vinegar in a large pan and bring to the boil.

4. Add the gherkins and remove the pan from the heat.

5. Allow the pickles to cool for 1 hour before bottling in sterile jars and sealing well.

Storage
Leave the gherkins for at least 1 month before eating. They should keep for 6–9 months unopened.

Pickled Nasturtium Seeds

These can be used as an alternative to capers. If you take the jar or jars you want to fill with the seeds with you when you pick them you will be able to see how many are needed. They are best picked on a dry day.

Nasturtium seeds
Spiced vinegar (see page 111)

For the brine
120g coarse salt
1 litre water

1. Wash the seeds well and steep them in a brine solution overnight (see page 113).

2. Drain and rinse under cold water.

3. Pack into sterile jars and cover with the vinegar.

Storage
Leave to mature for 4 weeks then use as you would capers.

Pickled Onions

3kg onions
(small pickling onions are best, available late August/early September)
At least 2 litres spiced vinegar (see page 111)

For the brine
120g coarse salt
1 litre water

1. Peel the onions and soak in a brine solution for 36 hours (see page 113).

2. Drain away all the brine and rinse the onions in cold water.

3. Pack into sterile jars and cover with cold vinegar.

Variation
Shallots may be used instead of onions.

Storage
Leave to mature for at least 2 months before serving. The pickled onions will keep for 12 months unopened. Once opened, store in the fridge and use within 3 weeks.

Pickled Sweet Peppers

1.5kg (approximately) red and green peppers
600ml spiced vinegar (see page 111)
50g white sugar
2–3 red chillies per jar
10–12 black peppercorns

1. Heat the vinegar in a pan and add the sugar. Stir until the sugar dissolves and the vinegar is hot.

2. Slice the peppers in half and deseed them. Chop into slices roughly 3cm long.

3. Have a pan of boiling water ready to blanch the peppers for 2 minutes. Lift them out of the water and pack into sterile jars, draining well of as much water as you can.

4. Add a few chillies and 5–6 black peppercorns to each jar.

5. Pour over the hot sweetened vinegar and seal well.

6. Label and date the jars.

Storage
This will be ready to eat in about 10 days. Use within 3 months if unopened. Once opened, refrigerate and use within 3 weeks.

Pickled Walnuts

Collect walnuts for pickling at the end of June or the beginning of July, while the nuts are still young. Always wear gloves, both for picking and pricking the walnuts, as the juice that comes out of them is dark brown and stains the fingers. It is very difficult to remove, so beware!

1kg walnuts
Spiced vinegar (see page 111)

For each brine solution (2 required)
300g coarse salt
1 litre water

1. Prick the walnuts with a large pin or needle and soak them in a brine solution for 48 hours (see page 113).

2. Drain and soak them for a second time in a fresh brine solution for 5 more days.

3. Drain and leave the walnuts exposed to the air for 24 hours or until they turn black.

4. Pack them into sterile jars and cover with sweet spiced vinegar. Seal immediately.

Storage
These will be ready for eating in about 5–6 weeks. They will keep for 4 months unopened. Once opened, refrigerate and use within 2 weeks.

Mixed pickle recipes

Onion, Cauliflower and Gherkin Pickle

3kg of pickling onions, cauliflower and gherkins in whatever proportion
you prefer
A dried red chilli for each jar
At least 2 litres of spiced vinegar (see page 111)

For the brine
300g coarse salt
1 litre water

1. Peel the onions, break the cauliflower into very small florets and chop the gherkins into 1cm slices or in half if they are very small.

2. Mix the vegetables together in a large bowl and cover with the brine solution (see page 113). Leave overnight to soak.

3. Drain away the brine and rinse the vegetables. Drain well.

4. Pack the vegetables into sterile jars, placing a dried chilli in amongst the other ingredients.

5. Pour over the spiced vinegar and seal the jars. Label and date the pickles.

Storage
These should be left to mature for 2 months before serving.

Onion and Cucumber Pickle

1kg pickling onions (small ones are best for this recipe)
2 large cucumbers
Coarse salt
Spiced vinegar (see page 111)

1. Peel the onions. Wash the skin of the cucumbers well and pat dry.

2. Slice the cucumbers into 1cm slices and layer with the onions in a dish, sprinkling each layer with coarse salt. Leave for 24 hours.

3. Drain off the salty liquor and rinse the onions and cucumber well in cold water. Drain again.

4. Pack into sterile jars and cover with the spiced vinegar.

5. Seal and label the jars.

Storage
This pickle will be ready to eat after 2 weeks.

Onion, Cauliflower, Bean and Marrow Pickle

*3kg of mixed vegetables: small onions, cauliflower, whole green beans
(preferably the dwarf type) and marrow
Coarse salt for the marrow
At least 2 litres of spiced vinegar (see page 111)*

For the brine
*120g coarse salt
1 litre water*

1. Cut the marrow flesh into about 1cm pieces and place in a dish, layering it with the salt.

2. Peel the onions and break the cauliflower into small florets. Cut the beans into 2cm pieces. Put the onions, cauliflower and beans in a brine solution (see page 113). Leave both the marrow and brined vegetables for 24 hours to steep.

3. Drain and rinse the vegetables and pack into sterile jars.

4. Pour over the spiced vinegar.

5. Seal and label the jars.

Storage
Leave to mature for 2–3 weeks before serving.

Cooked pickle recipes

Pickled Beetroot

2kg beetroot, unpeeled
Spiced vinegar (see page 111)
1 level tablespoon white sugar (you may omit this if you prefer the
vinegar unsweetened)

1. Wash the beetroot without rupturing the skin. Place in a pan containing sufficient boiling water to cover it, and to which ½ teaspoon of salt has been added. Boil for about 1½ hours.

2. Leave to cool and then rub off the skins. Use rubber gloves for this, not only to protect your hands from staining but also because they will help to remove the skins more easily.

3. While the beetroot is cooling, heat the vinegar in a pan and stir in the sugar if using. Keep the vinegar hot until you are ready to pour it over the beetroot.

4. When cool, either cut the beetroot into slices about 5mm thick or dice into small cubes. Pack into sterile jars and pour over the hot spiced vinegar.

5. Seal the jars immediately. Label when the jars are cool.

Storage
This can be eaten after 2–3 days. It will keep for 2 months unopened. Once opened, store in the fridge and use within 2 weeks.

Pickled Cauliflower

1 large cauliflower
Spiced vinegar (see page 111)
½ teaspoon each of salt and ground black pepper

1. Break the cauliflower into small florets and boil in salted water for about 5 minutes. Drain well.

2. Put back in the pan and pour over the vinegar. Bring to the boil and add the salt and pepper. When the liquid is boiling remove the pan from the heat, cover and allow the cauliflower to cool.

3. When cool, drain the cauliflower, reserving all the vinegar. Pack into sterile jars and pour over the vinegar.

4. Seal immediately and label the jars.

Storage
Leave for 2–3 days before eating. This can be stored for up to 6 months unopened. Once opened, store in the fridge and use within 4 weeks.

Sweetened vegetable pickle recipes
(and those that don't use the spiced vinegar)

Pickled Carrots

I find these taste better if you use distilled white vinegar and add the spices just before you make your pickles.

1kg small carrots
About 700ml white distilled vinegar
Pickling spices for mild pickles (see page 110) tied in a muslin bag
1 level teaspoon salt
100g white sugar

1. Wash and scrub or peel the carrots. Simmer in slightly salted water for 10 minutes and drain.

2. Put the vinegar, spices and salt in a pan and bring to the boil. Boil the vinegar for 10 minutes.

3. Remove from the heat and take out the muslin bag with tongs, squeezing out any dregs of vinegar.

4. Add the sugar and stir well.

5. Add the carrots and boil everything together for about 5–10 minutes or until the carrots are just tender.

6. Transfer the carrots to hot sterile jars and pour over the vinegar left in the pan. Seal immediately. Label when the jars are cool.

Storage
Leave for 2–3 days before eating. This will keep for up to 6 months unopened. Once opened, store in the fridge and use within 4 weeks.

Pickled Marrow

Pickled marrow makes an excellent accompaniment to curries as an
alternative to mango chutney.

2kg marrow, after peeling and deseeding
Coarse salt
1 litre distilled white vinegar
1 rounded teaspoon ground ginger
1 rounded teaspoon medium curry powder
30g dry mustard
10 black peppercorns
250g white sugar

1. Peel, deseed and chop the marrow into small cubes. Place in a dish
and sprinkle with the salt. Leave overnight or for at least 6 hours.

2. Just before you rinse the marrow of the salt, put the vinegar in a
pan, add the spices, mustard and peppercorns and bring to the boil.

3. When the vinegar is boiling, remove from the heat and stir in the
sugar. Return the pan to the heat and stir until the sugar has dissolved.

4. Bring back to the boil and boil for 5 minutes.

5. Drain and rinse the marrow and add to the vinegar. It is easiest if
you remove the pan from the heat before adding the marrow.

6. Simmer – don't boil – the mixture until the marrow is just tender.

7. Pour the hot mixture into hot sterile jars and seal immediately.

Storage
The pickle will be ready to eat in about 2 weeks.

Pickled Mushrooms

You would not normally associate mushrooms with pickling but these are really very good.

500g mushrooms (small closed cup ones are best)
280ml white wine vinegar
6 black peppercorns
½ teaspoon ground ginger
1 level teaspoon salt
2–3 cloves garlic, peeled and cut in half
A pinch nutmeg
Sunflower oil (see method for amount)

1. Wipe the mushrooms with a damp cloth to remove any debris.

2. Put the vinegar in a pan with the peppercorns, ginger, salt, garlic and nutmeg and bring to the boil.

3. Add the mushrooms as soon as the vinegar is boiling then reduce the heat to a simmer and cook for about 8 minutes or until the mushrooms are tender to your taste.

4. Transfer the mushrooms to a hot sterile jar and top up with the rest of the vinegar to about 2cm from the top of the jar. Remove the garlic from the vinegar first.

5. Pour a 1cm layer of oil onto the vinegar and seal well immediately. Label when cool.

Storage
Leave for 2 weeks to mature.

Blended pickle recipes

These are finer pickles, where the vegetables have been chopped
and cooked with vinegar, sugar and spices, like the popular
Mustard Pickle.

Celery, Cucumber and Courgette Pickle

Pick your marrows when they are small to make this pickle.

2 cucumbers
4–5 courgettes
4 sticks celery
1 medium-sized onion
1 tablespoon coarse salt
2 tablespoons cornflour
300ml cider vinegar
1 teaspoon turmeric
50g dry mustard
130g white sugar, or soft brown sugar for more of a caramel flavour

1. Peel and cube the cucumbers and courgettes and chop the celery.
Peel and chop the onion finely. Mix all the vegetables together and
place in a dish, spreading them out thinly. Sprinkle with the coarse
salt and leave to one side for about 30 minutes.

2. Mix the cornflour with 2 tablespoons of vinegar to make a smooth
paste.

3. Put the vinegar in a pan with the turmeric, mustard and sugar and
place over a low heat.

4. Whisk the cornflour mixture into the vinegar. Stir constantly until the mixture is almost boiling then simmer for 3 minutes.

5. Drain the vegetables of the liquor, rinse quickly and drain again.

6. Add the vegetables to the vinegar and simmer for about 30 minutes or until the pickle is thick. Stir now and again to keep the mixture from catching.

7. Pour into hot sterile jars and seal. Label when cool.

Storage
Leave to mature for 2 weeks.

Mustard Pickle

1 cucumber, peeled if you prefer, and diced
2 medium-sized onions, finely chopped
1 small cauliflower, broken into small florets
2 large green peppers, chopped
350g of either young runner beans or dwarf beans, sliced into 1cm pieces
350g gherkins, thickly sliced
350g green or under-ripe tomatoes, chopped
100g coarse salt
Water to just cover
1.3 litres distilled white vinegar
30g mustard seeds
300g white sugar
2 rounded tablespoons plain flour
25g dry mustard
1 teaspoon turmeric

1. Mix all the vegetables together in a large bowl, sprinkle over the salt and pour over the water. Leave to soak for 8 hours.

2. Drain the vegetables well and rinse quickly under cold water. Drain again.

3. Put the vinegar in the pan except for 3 tablespoons; set this aside for mixing with the flour and mustard.

4. Add the mustard seeds and sugar to the vinegar and stir over a low heat until all the sugar has dissolved.

5. Add the vegetables and bring to the boil. Boil vigorously for 5 minutes then turn down the heat to a fast simmer. Continue to simmer for 15 minutes. Test to see if there is enough salt in the mixture; it should contain some of the brine solution.

6. Make a smooth paste with the flour, mustard powder, turmeric and set aside vinegar and stir this into the simmering mixture.

7. Continue simmering for about 10 more minutes, stirring every few minutes.

8. Pot into warm sterile jars and seal.

9. Label and date the jars when cool.

Storage
Allow to mature for 4 weeks before consuming.

Piccalilli

This is a great way to use up your end-of-season vegetables, such as cucumber, gherkins, marrow, courgettes and green beans. Small cauliflowers that haven't grown well are ideal for this recipe and unripened tomatoes and small onions can all be used. The method is the same whether you make hot, tangy piccalilli or a milder version.

MAKES ABOUT 6 X 500G JARS

3kg mixed vegetables, cut into small, fairly even-sized pieces
450g cooking salt

For hot, tangy piccalilli
1 level tablespoon turmeric
3 level tablespoons dry mustard
6 level tablespoons ground ginger
180g white sugar
1 litre distilled white vinegar
1 rounded tablespoon cornflour, mixed to a smooth paste with
2 tablespoons of the vinegar

For milder, sweeter piccalilli
1 level teaspoon turmeric
4 teaspoons dry mustard
3 teaspoons ground ginger
280g white sugar
1 litre distilled white vinegar
1 rounded tablespoon cornflour, mixed to a smooth paste with
2 tablespoons of the vinegar

1. Lay the vegetables in a large dish and sprinkle the cooking salt liberally over them. Leave for at least 8 hours. Then drain and rinse them.

2. Mix the turmeric, mustard, ginger and sugar together.

3. Put the vegetables in a large pan. Pour over half of the vinegar and stir the spices and sugar into the other half then stir into the vegetables.

4. Bring to the boil then turn down the heat to a simmer. For a crisp vegetable texture, simmer for about 20 minutes. For a softer vegetable, simmer for about 30 minutes.

5. Stir in the cornflour paste and bring the mixture to the boil. Continue to boil for 1–2 minutes, stirring gently, to cook the flour.

6. Ladle carefully into sterile jars and seal immediately.

7. Label and date the jars when cool.

Storage
Leave to mature for 4 weeks.

Brown Pickle

This is one of our family favourites. I make this with all sorts of
vegetables, depending on what is available. The pickle keeps well
even when opened so long as it is stored in the fridge. It can be
eaten with cheese, cooked meats and salads. My corned beef
sandwich just wouldn't be the same without it! The vegetables can
be chopped as finely as you wish; if you like a very fine-textured
pickle they can be chopped in a food processor.

MAKES 4 X 450G JARS

250g carrots
1 medium swede
4 cloves garlic, chopped
125g dates, finely chopped
2 onions
2 medium apples, dessert or cooking (dessert apples give a sweeter
flavour); no need to peel, just dice
15 small gherkins or a medium-sized cucumber cut into small cubes
250g brown sugar
1 teaspoon salt
2 teaspoons mustard seeds
2 teaspoons allspice
4 tablespoons lemon juice
500ml malt vinegar

1. Put all the ingredients into a large pan and stir well.

2. Bring to the boil, stirring constantly.

3. Reduce the heat to a gentle simmer and maintain this for 2 hours, stirring every 20 minutes or so.

4. The pickle should look moist but not wet or runny.

5. Ladle into sterile jars and seal immediately.

Storage
This should be left to mature for about 5 days before consuming. However, if you can leave it for at least a week, the flavour will be even better.

Fruit pickle recipes

I love fruit pickles with cheese, especially a creamy cheese like Brie.
Some can be eaten as a dessert with cream. Use the sweet vinegar
recipe for these pickles, but use white or white wine vinegar, not malt.

Apple Pickle

1kg cooking apples
600ml sweet, spiced white wine vinegar (see page 111)
800g white sugar

1. Put the vinegar in a pan and stir in the sugar. Bring slowly to
simmering, stirring constantly until the sugar has dissolved. Bring to
the boil and boil for 5 minutes. Remove from the heat.

2. Peel, core and dice or slice the apples, whichever you prefer, and
put the fruit in the hot vinegar.

3. Bring to the boil and turn down the heat to simmering. Simmer for
about 15 minutes or until the fruit is tender.

4. Lift the fruit out of the vinegar and spoon into the sterile jars.

5. Bring the vinegar syrup back to the boil and reduce by about half.

6. Pour over the fruit and seal immediately.

7. Label and date the jars when cool.

Storage
Leave the pickle for 2 weeks before eating.

Apricot Pickle

This can be eaten with cream or used as a base for winter fruit salad. It is quick and easy to prepare and a wonderful way to preserve your harvest of apricots.

1kg apricots
450ml sweet, spiced white wine vinegar (see page 111)
1kg white sugar

1. Preheat the oven to 180°C/gas mark 4.

2. Cut the apricots in half and remove the stones.

3. Place them in a dish or roasting pan, cover with a lid or foil and place in the preheated oven for 15 minutes. After this time the skins should be beginning to peel away from the flesh.

4. Take the apricots out of the oven and remove the skins. Pack them in hot sterile jars.

5. Put the vinegar in a pan and stir in the sugar. Place on a low heat and stir until the sugar has dissolved.

6. Bring the vinegar to boiling then pour over the apricots. Seal the jars immediately.

7. Label and date the jars when cool.

Variation
Use peaches instead of the apricots to make Peach Pickle.

Storage
Leave for at least 3 weeks before eating.

Blackberry Pickle

1kg blackberries, washed and hulled
300ml white vinegar
500g white sugar
1 level teaspoon allspice
1 level teaspoon ground cinnamon

1. Heat the vinegar in a large pan and slowly dissolve the sugar, stirring continuously.

2. Bring the syrup to the boil and add the blackberries. Cover and simmer for about 10 minutes or until the fruit is tender.

3. Remove the blackberries and pack into sterile jars. The easiest way to do this is by pouring the syrup into another pan, retaining the blackberries, and then spooning the fruit into the prepared jars.

4. Add the spices to the vinegar syrup and stir well. Bring to the boil and reduce until the mixture has thickened; this will take about 15 minutes.

5. Pour the syrup over the fruit and seal immediately.

6. Label and date the jars when cool.

Variation
Use blackcurrants instead of the blackberries. They will take about 25 minutes to cook in the syrup at step 2.

Storage
Leave to mature for 4 weeks before eating.

Crab Apple Pickle

2kg good-quality crab apples
Juice of ½ lemon
Water to just cover
600ml white vinegar
1.25kg sugar
2cm piece of fresh ginger
1 cinnamon stick

1. Wash the fruit and put in a pan with the lemon juice and enough water to just cover. Bring to the boil then simmer for about 20 minutes or until just tender.

2. Lift the fruit out of the water and leave to drain well. Reserve 350ml of the cooking liquid.

3. Put the vinegar in a pan with the cooking liquid and add the sugar. Place over a low heat and add the spices. Stir until all the sugar has dissolved.

4. Bring the syrup to the boil then turn down and simmer for 5 minutes.

5. Put the apples back in the simmering syrup and cook for 5 more minutes at a fast simmer.

6. Remove the apples from the syrup and spoon into hot sterile jars.

7. Boil the syrup until it thickens and is reduced by about a third. Pour over the apples and seal immediately.

8. Label and date the jars when cool.

Storage
Allow to stand for 4 weeks before eating.

Gooseberry Pickle

2.5kg gooseberries (choose firm, slightly under-ripe fruit)
1 litre sweet, spiced white wine vinegar (see page 111)
1.5kg sugar

1. Top and tail the gooseberries and wash well.

2. Pour the vinegar into a pan, place over a low heat and stir in the sugar. Continue to stir until the sugar has dissolved.

3. Add the gooseberries and cover. Simmer for about 15 minutes or until the gooseberries are tender.

4. Lift the gooseberries out of the syrup and pack into sterile jars.

5. Bring the syrup to the boil and reduce until very thick. Pour over the fruit and seal immediately.

6. Label and date the jars when cool.

Storage
Allow this to stand for 6 weeks before eating.

Pear Pickle

2kg pears (choose very firm, under-ripe eating pears of any type)
1kg sugar
600ml sweet, spiced white vinegar (see page 111)

1. Put the sugar and vinegar together in a pan over a low heat and stir until all the sugar has dissolved. Bring to the boil and boil for 10 minutes.

2. While the syrup is boiling, peel, core and quarter the pears.

3. Remove the syrup from the heat. Put the fruit into the syrup and bring back to the boil.

4. Turn down the heat to a gentle simmer and cover and simmer until the pears are tender; this will take about 10 minutes.

5. Lift the pears out of the syrup and pack into the sterile jars.

6. Boil the syrup again then pour over the fruit.

7. Seal the jars and label and date when cool.

Storage
Leave to stand for 3 weeks before eating.

Plum Pickle

These are best made using the whole fruit. Choose firm, medium-sized fruits with no bruising or soft bits. Simply remove the stalks and wash and dry the plums.

1.5kg plums (Victorias are the best or any other British-grown variety)
1.25kg sugar
700ml sweet, spiced white vinegar (see page 111)
Zest and juice of 1 lemon

1. Prick the plums all over.

2. Put the sugar and vinegar together in a pan and stir over a low heat until all the sugar has dissolved. Bring to the boil then turn down the heat to simmering and add the plums. Continue to simmer until the fruit is tender; this will take about 15 minutes.

3. Remove the fruit from the syrup and pack into hot sterile jars.

4. Bring the syrup back to the boil then reduce until thick.

5. Pour over the fruit and seal immediately.

6. Label and date the jars when cool.

Storage
Leave to stand for 6 weeks before eating.

10. Making Chutney and Relishes

Chutney

Making chutney is easy, although slightly more time-consuming than other preserves to prepare, as the vegetables and fruit need to be finely chopped. However, a food processor will speed this up if you have one. And in any case the texture of the chutney is a matter of choice; you may prefer to leave the fruit and vegetables chunky. Adjust the sizes according to your taste. The larger pieces will obviously take longer to cook. As with most of the recipes in this book, all the ingredients are cooked together.

Try making small batches of a new chutney recipe to begin with; this way you can adjust the seasonings to your own taste. Do allow the chutney the allotted time to mature before you taste it so that you get the best possible indication of the final flavour.

Three steps to great chutney

There are only three steps in the making of chutney, listed below.

Step 1: Prepare the ingredients
Step 2: Bring the mixture to the boil then simmer the ingredients

Some recipes just bring to a simmer without boiling. Do not cover unless the recipe asks for this as the liquid needs to evaporate in order to allow the chutney to thicken sufficiently.

Step 3: Pot the chutney

Yields

So far as the yield is concerned, an approximate amount is given with each recipe. These are always overestimated so that you will have sufficient pots ready to take the chutney.

Storage

Chutney should be stored in a cool, dark place and should keep for at least 12 months unopened. The recipe will indicate if the chutney should be stored differently. Once opened, store in the fridge and consume within 4 weeks.

While you are storing your chutneys keep checking that they are not shrinking away from the jars. This happens when there is a poor seal on the jar and liquid has evaporated from the chutney. Unfortunately, if this happens your chutney will be inedible. Sealing the jars is therefore of the utmost importance, as with other preserves.

Apple Chutneys

Apples are very useful for making chutneys and I use them in many recipes. You can make them as spicy as you wish; we don't like them too spicy, so these are mild to medium flavoured depending on the quantity of spices you want to use. The longer they are left to mature after potting, the mellower the flavour. Each recipe gives the optimum time for the chutney to mature.

Simple Apple Chutney

Use malt vinegar if you prefer darker brown chutney, white for a
lighter colour and milder taste.

MAKES ABOUT 8 X 500G JARS

1kg onions
3kg apples (a mixture of dessert and cooking is good)
25–30g salt, depending on how salty you like your chutney
20–25g ground ginger
1½–2 level tablespoons ground cinnamon
1 litre malt or distilled white vinegar
150ml water
1kg soft brown or granulated white sugar
3 tablespoons honey

1. Peel and chop the onions finely. Peel and core the apples and chop
into small pieces.

2. Place the apples and onions in a large preserving pan and add all
the other ingredients.

3. Stir over a low heat until the sugar dissolves. Raise the heat and
bring slowly to the boil.

4. Reduce the heat and simmer for about 1½ hours or until the
mixture is thick and smooth. Stir regularly.

5. Pot into sterile jars while the chutney is still very hot, and seal.
Allow the jars to cool before labelling.

Storage
Allow this to mature for at least 6 weeks before eating.

Apple and Beetroot Chutney

A richly coloured chutney, this is excellent with roast pork or goose
instead of apple sauce.

MAKES ABOUT 5 X 500G JARS

1kg beetroot (use uncooked)
700g cooking apples
500g onions, finely chopped
500g raisins
1 tablespoon mixed spice
1 teaspoon ground ginger
1 litre malt vinegar
1kg soft brown sugar

1. Peel and grate the beetroot and place in a pan.

2. Core and chop the apples, peel if you wish, and place in the pan
with the beetroot.

3. Add all the other ingredients and stir over a low heat until the sugar
dissolves.

4. Bring slowly to the boil, stirring continuously.

5. Reduce the heat and simmer for about 1 hour or until the chutney
is thick and smooth.

6. Ladle immediately into sterile jars and seal well. Allow to cool
before labelling the jars.

Storage
Allow to mature for 4 weeks before eating.

Apple and Cranberry Chutney

This is a wonderful preserve that can be eaten at any time of the year, not just at Christmas. Try it on a toasted cheese sandwich, using Stilton or mature Cheddar. Amazing!

MAKES ABOUT 5 X 500G JARS

1kg apples
1kg cranberries
1 medium-sized onion
700ml vinegar
700g sugar
1 teaspoon each of ground ginger and allspice
A pinch each of freshly grated nutmeg and ground cloves
2 rounded teaspoons salt
Grated zest of 1 orange
3 tablespoons orange juice

1. Peel, core and chop the apples and place in a pan with the cranberries.

2. Add all the other ingredients and stir over a low heat until the sugar has dissolved.

3. Bring to the boil then reduce the heat and simmer for about 1½ hours.

4. The chutney should look thick and smooth with very little liquid left when it is ready.

5. Ladle immediately into sterile jars, sealing well. Label when cool.

Storage
Allow to mature for 4 weeks before eating.

Apple, Pepper and Marrow Chutney

This is a great accompaniment to kormas and other mild curry dishes.

MAKES ABOUT 5 x 500G JARS

550–600g or 2 large cooking apples
4 red peppers, chopped
½ small marrow, peeled and cubed
2 medium onions, finely chopped
2 cloves garlic, crushed or chopped
1 level teaspoon turmeric
1 level teaspoon cumin
1 level teaspoon mild curry powder
2 level teaspoons salt
180g raisins
1–2 small red chillies, chopped
350g soft brown sugar
650ml spiced pickling vinegar (see page 111)

1. Peel, core and chop the apples and put into a large preserving pan.

2. Add all the other ingredients and stir over a low heat until all the sugar has dissolved.

3. Bring to the boil, stirring constantly, then reduce the heat and simmer for about 1½ hours or until the chutney is thick and smooth.

4. Ladle into the prepared jars and seal well.

5. Label the jars when cool.

Storage
Leave to mature for 6 weeks before eating.

Apple and Sultana Chutney

This is a real favourite of mine; I enjoy eating it with cheese
and crackers.

MAKES ABOUT 7 X 500G JARS

3.5kg apples
500g sultanas
3 cloves garlic, crushed
1 litre vinegar, malt or white
1.5kg sugar
1 rounded teaspoon ground ginger
2 rounded teaspoons ground cinnamon
2–3 teaspoons salt

1. Peel, core and chop the apples and place in a pan with the other
ingredients.

2. Stir over a low heat until the sugar dissolves.

3. Raise the heat to simmering and cook for about 2 hours, stirring
occasionally.

4. When the mixture looks thick and smooth, ladle into the prepared
jars. Seal immediately.

Storage
Allow to mature for 4–6 weeks before eating.

Autumn Fruit Chutney

This is a great way to use up fruit from the orchard. It is a mild
fruity chutney that can be used for all cheeses and cooked meats,
but I really enjoy a spoonful with a Cornish pasty.

MAKES ABOUT 4 X 500G JARS

1.5kg mixed apples, pears and plums
100g chopped dates
100g raisins
400g onions, finely chopped
300g soft brown sugar
580ml malt vinegar
1 teaspoon each of ground allspice, ginger and salt

1. Peel and core or stone the fruit and chop up finely.

2. Put all the ingredients together in a large pan and heat gently,
stirring continuously until the sugar has dissolved.

3. Raise the heat to simmering and cook for about 1½ hours until the
chutney is smooth and thick.

4. Ladle into prepared jars and seal immediately. Label when the jars
are cool.

Storage
Allow to mature for 6 weeks before eating.

Dried Fruit Chutney

MAKES ABOUT 2 X 500G JARS

1kg mixed dried fruit: sultanas, apples, apricots, peaches, pears, raisins
500ml white vinegar
250g soft brown sugar
1 teaspoon mixed spice
½ teaspoon ground cinnamon
½ teaspoon ground cloves
1 teaspoon salt

1. Put the vinegar and sugar in a pan with the spices and salt. Heat gently, stirring continuously until the sugar has dissolved.

2. Bring the vinegar mixture to the boil then remove from the heat.

3. Add the dried fruit and stir well. Leave for 30 minutes.

4. Return to the heat and bring the mixture to a fast simmer.

5. Reduce the heat to a gentle simmer and leave to cook for about 1½ hours or until the chutney is thick and the fruit very soft, stirring from time to time.

6. Ladle into prepared jars and seal immediately.

Storage
Allow to mature for 4 weeks before eating.

Gooseberry Chutney

This has a sharp, clean taste that goes well with spicy dishes.

MAKES ABOUT 4 X 50G JARS

1.5kg gooseberries
200g onions, finely chopped
200g sultanas
150g chopped dates
250g sugar
580ml white vinegar
1 teaspoon salt
1 teaspoon ground ginger
1 teaspoon mixed spice

1. Wash and top and tail the fruit and place in a pan with the onions.

2. Add the rest of the ingredients and stir over a low heat until all the sugar has dissolved.

3. Raise the heat and bring the mixture to the boil, reduce the heat to simmering and cook for 1½ hours or until the chutney is thick and smooth.

4. Ladle into prepared jars and seal immediately. Label when cool.

Storage
Allow to mature for 3 weeks before eating.

Green Tomato Chutney

This can also be made with red tomatoes. If your tomatoes are very ripe, reduce the amount of sugar to 400g to balance the sweetness.

MAKES ABOUT 5 X 500G JARS

2kg green tomatoes
700g onions, finely chopped
450g Bramley or other cooking apples, peeled, cored and chopped
200g raisins
500g golden caster sugar
600ml white vinegar
25g fresh root ginger, finely chopped
1 level teaspoon mixed spice
2 teaspoons salt

1. Chop the tomatoes and place in a pan with the other ingredients.

2. Heat gently, stirring until all the sugar has dissolved.

3. Raise the heat and bring to the boil then simmer for 1½ hours until the chutney is thick and smooth.

4. Ladle into prepared jars and seal immediately. Label when cool.

Variation
For a spicier chutney, omit the mixed spice and add ½–1 teaspoon hot chilli powder or dried chillies, 2 grated garlic cloves and 2 teaspoons curry powder.

Storage
For the best flavour, allow to mature for 4–5 weeks before eating.

Lime Chutney

MAKES ABOUT 2 X 500G JARS

12 limes
2 cloves garlic, chopped or grated
10g fresh ginger, chopped
5 green chillies, finely chopped
180g soft brown sugar
200ml white vinegar

1. If the limes are unwaxed give them a quick wash; if not, use warm soapy water and scrub them gently with a pan scourer. Rinse in cold water.

2. Chop the limes into small chunks, catching all the juice in a dish to add to the chutney.

3. Mix together all the ingredients in a large preserving pan and heat to simmering, stirring all the time as the sugar dissolves.

4. Simmer for 1–1½ hours or until the chutney thickens.

5. Pot into prepared jars and seal. Label the jars when cool.

Storage
Allow to mature for 3 weeks before eating.

Mango Chutney

This is well known as a classic accompaniment to Indian dishes, but a friend has passed on to me the following idea for a delicious sandwich filling: combine a good-sized portion of cooked cold chicken with a dessert spoon of mango chutney, pop it between two slices of your favourite bread and enjoy.

MAKES 2 X 500G JARS

3 under-ripe mangoes, peeled and diced into small pieces
2 teaspoons salt
3 cloves garlic, finely chopped
10g fresh ginger, chopped or grated
½ teaspoon turmeric
½ level teaspoon cayenne pepper
1 teaspoon salt
350g soft brown sugar
350ml white vinegar

1. Put the mangoes in a dish and sprinkle with the 2 teaspoons salt. Cover and leave overnight. The next day, drain and rinse the mangoes and then drain again.

2. Put the mangoes in a pan with all the other ingredients and heat gently, stirring all the time until the sugar has dissolved.

3. Simmer for about 30–40 minutes until the mixture thickens.

4. Ladle into prepared jars and seal immediately. Label when cool.

Storage
Leave to mature for 7 days before eating.

Vegetable chutneys

Quick Red Onion Chutney

This is ready to eat as soon as it is cold. It is delicious with burgers and sausages and great in a cheese tart.

MAKES 1 X 350G JAR

3 medium-sized red onions, finely chopped or sliced
5 rounded tablespoons soft brown sugar
100ml white wine vinegar
½ teaspoon salt
½ teaspoon ground cinnamon

1. Put all the ingredients into a pan over a low heat and stir until all the sugar has dissolved.

2. Bring to the boil and then reduce the heat and simmer for about 40 minutes, stirring occasionally. The finished chutney should be thick but moist-looking.

3. Stir then pot into prepared jars and cover well. Label when cool.

Storage and serving
This chutney can be eaten as soon as it is cold but will taste better if you leave it for 24 hours. If you are saving it for a later date, secure with a well-fitting lid and store in the fridge. Stored in this way, it will keep for up to 6 months. Once opened, eat within 4 weeks.

Roasted Red Pepper and Tomato Chutney

MAKES ABOUT 3 X 500G JARS

4 large red peppers
1 tablespoon oil
1kg tomatoes, chopped
2 large onions, finely chopped
1 red chilli, chopped, or ½–1 teaspoon dried chillies
400g golden caster sugar
580ml white wine vinegar
½ teaspoon paprika
1 teaspoon salt

1. Preheat the oven to 200°C/gas mark 6.

2. Cut the peppers in half and remove the stalks and seeds. Place on a lightly oiled baking tray and coat the peppers with the oil. Roast for 15–20 minutes until parts of the peppers are beginning to brown.

3. Meanwhile put all the other ingredients in a large pan and heat gently, stirring until all the sugar has dissolved. Once all the sugar has dissolved, bring the mixture to the boil and then reduce the heat to a simmer.

4. When the peppers are ready, remove them from the oven. Peel the skins away from them if you wish, then chop into small pieces.

5. Stir the peppers into the simmering mixture and continue to cook for 1½ hours until thick.

6. Ladle into prepared jars and seal immediately. Label when cool.

Storage
This can be eaten after 3 days.

Mixed Pepper Chutney

MAKES ABOUT 3 X 500G JARS

2 each of red, green and yellow or orange peppers, chopped
400g tomatoes (under-ripe or still green are best)
350g onions, finely chopped
350g soft brown sugar
450ml white wine vinegar
1 teaspoon allspice
1 teaspoon mustard powder
2 level teaspoons salt
¼ teaspoon white pepper

1. Put all the ingredients in a large preserving pan and heat gently, stirring until all the sugar has dissolved.

2. Bring to the boil then reduce the heat and simmer for 1½ hours or until thick.

3. Ladle into prepared jars and seal immediately. Label when cool.

Pumpkin Chutney

A sweet and spicy chutney, this goes well with cold meats and cheese.

MAKES ABOUT 4 X 500G JARS

1.5kg pumpkin, diced
400g tomatoes, chopped
250g onions, finely chopped
50g sultanas
600g soft brown sugar
600ml white vinegar
2 cloves garlic, chopped
2 level teaspoons allspice
½ teaspoon black pepper
1 teaspoon ground ginger
2 rounded teaspoons salt

1. Put all the ingredients together in a large preserving pan and stir over a low heat until the sugar has dissolved.

2. Bring everything to the boil then reduce the heat and simmer for 1 hour or until thick.

3. Pot and seal immediately and label when cool.

Storage
Store for 4–5 weeks before eating to allow the spices to mellow in the chutney.

Runner Bean Chutney

If, like us, you always seem to have far too many runner beans at any one time, this recipe offers you an unusual way of preserving them. I like to serve this chutney with heavily spiced dishes like rogan josh or a Madras curry.

MAKES ABOUT 4 X 500G JARS

1kg runner beans, cut into 1cm pieces
700g onions
700g soft brown sugar
700ml white vinegar
½–1 teaspoon salt
1 teaspoon turmeric
1 teaspoon ground cumin
½–1 teaspoon dry mustard

1. Put the runner beans in a saucepan and cover with sufficient salted hot water to just cover.

2. Bring to the boil then simmer for 8–10 minutes.

3. In a preserving pan mix all the other ingredients together and stir over a low heat until the sugar has dissolved.

4. Bring to the boil and simmer for 20 minutes.

5. Drain the beans as soon as they are cooked and add to the vinegar mixture after it has simmered for 20 minutes.

6. Allow the mixture to simmer steadily for another 20 minutes or until it has thickened.

7. Ladle the chutney into prepared jars and seal immediately. Label when cool.

Storage
This can be eaten after a few days, but try to leave it for 3–4 days to allow the flavours to settle.

Relishes

These are not as long-lasting as chutneys and pickles so are best made in smaller quantities, but will keep for 2–3 weeks in a well-sealed sterile jar. They add variety and taste to picnics and party food. They can be eaten as soon as they are cool, so there is no waiting for them to mature.

Fruit and vegetables need to be chopped very finely for relishes. This can be done by hand or in a food processor, although the food processor can sometimes chop them too finely. I find my small mincer does the quickest and best job.

Beetroot Relish

This is great with meat and potato pie or corned beef hash.

MAKES 1 x 700G JAR

500g beetroot, peeled and grated
250g white caster sugar
250ml cider vinegar
½ teaspoon salt
½ teaspoon chilli powder or a small chopped chilli

1. Put all the ingredients together in a pan and heat slowly, stirring constantly until all the sugar has dissolved.

2. Bring to the boil then reduce the heat to a gentle simmer and cook for 25–30 minutes or until the mixture is thick yet moist.

3. Ladle immediately into a prepared jar and allow to cool before using.

Serving
To achieve the full flavour of this relish serve completely cold.

Burger Relish

This is one to serve at barbecue time, but I always have a batch
ready for bonfire night as well.

MAKES 1 X 450G JAR

250g tomatoes, chopped
2 red peppers, finely chopped
1 onion, finely chopped
½ teaspoon chilli flakes, or 1 small red chilli, chopped
200g white caster sugar
200ml white wine vinegar
½ teaspoon salt
2 tablespoons tomato purée

1. Put all the ingredients into a pan and heat gently until the sugar
has dissolved.

2. Bring to the boil then reduce the heat to simmering and cook for
30 minutes.

3. Ladle immediately into a prepared jar.

Serving
Serve when completely cold.

Corn Relish

This is another favourite with burgers, but I also serve it with chicken and ham pie; the combination of chicken and sweetcorn is always a winner.

MAKES 1 X 500G JAR

400g can sweetcorn (or frozen if you prefer)
1 small onion, finely chopped
1 small red pepper, finely chopped
180g white caster sugar
200ml white wine vinegar
½ teaspoon turmeric
1 level teaspoon mustard powder
1 teaspoon salt
1 rounded teaspoon cornflour mixed with 2–3 teaspoons of the vinegar
to make a paste

1. Drain or defrost the sweetcorn and place in a pan with all the other ingredients. Stir over a low heat until all the sugar has dissolved.

2. Bring to the boil then simmer for 15–20 minutes or until the onion and pepper are tender and the relish is thick.

3. Ladle immediately into a prepared jar and allow to cool completely before serving.

Tomato Relish

150ml white wine vinegar
180g caster sugar
1 teaspoon mustard seeds
1 teaspoon salt
1 large onion, finely chopped
1 small red pepper, chopped
1 stick of celery, finely chopped
750g tomatoes, chopped
½ teaspoon chilli flakes, or 1 fresh chilli, chopped

1. Gently heat the vinegar, sugar, mustard seeds and salt in a pan, stirring until all the sugar dissolves.

2. Add the onion, pepper and celery and bring to the boil. Reduce the heat to simmering and cook for 10 minutes.

3. Add the tomatoes and chilli and simmer for 20–25 more minutes or until the mixture thickens.

4. Stir and ladle immediately into prepared jars.

Serving
Leave to cool completely before eating.

11. Making Ketchups, Sauces and Flavoured Vinegars

Most food is enhanced by the addition of an accompaniment. Roast pork or goose and apple sauce, sausages with brown sauce or tomato ketchup, roast lamb and mint sauce are all classic examples of marrying food flavours together.

Ketchups and sauces

These don't keep for as long as chutneys or jams as they are not boiled for long enough; boiling spoils the flavour of the finished product. However, the bottles may be sterilised after filling.

Home-made sauces and ketchups are very easy to make. The only time-consuming step is rubbing the pulp through a sieve. This is best done using a good sieve and a wooden spoon to push through the pulp; you will then get most of the pulp as well as the juice.

Sterilising the ketchups and sauces

Once you have bottled your ketchups and sauces you can sterilise the bottles. Place a piece of wood at the bottom of a large pan, loosen the lids slightly and stand the bottles on the wood. Add sufficient warm, not boiling, water to reach the tops of the bottles, about 2cm away from the lids. Use a preserving thermometer to measure the temperature of the water as it heats; it needs to reach 78°C/170°F. Keep this temperature constant for 30 minutes. Then remove the bottles from the pan, taking care not to burn your hands, and screw the tops on tightly. The ketchups and sauces will keep for up to 6 months. All can be used as soon as they are cold.

Tomato Ketchup

This is probably one of the most popular accompaniments to all kinds of foods, especially among children, who seem to want to eat it with almost everything. So it's a real bonus to be able to make your own and know exactly what is going into it. Use wide-necked bottles with well-fitting screw-top lids for this recipe and use a sterile funnel for ease of pouring.

MAKES ABOUT 1 LITRE

500ml white vinegar
2 level teaspoons pickling spices
3kg ripe tomatoes, sliced
1 large onion, finely chopped
2 Bramley or other cooking apples, peeled and diced
180g sugar
½ teaspoon paprika
3 teaspoons salt

1. Put the vinegar in a pan with the pickling spices and bring to the boil. Boil for 10 minutes then remove from the heat, leave for 10 minutes and then strain off the spices. This will give just enough of a hint of spice in the ketchup.

2. In a large pan stir together the tomatoes, onion and apples and simmer for about 20 minutes until everything is pulpy and soft.

3. Sieve the pulp and return it to the pan.

4. Stir in the vinegar, sugar, paprika and salt and bring to a fast simmer.

5. Simmer until the mixture is the consistency of double cream.

6. Pour into warm sterile bottles and secure the lids.

7. Label and date when cool.

Storage
This will keep for 4 weeks in the fridge but, once opened, consume within a week. Alternatively, for a longer shelf life, sterilise the bottles once you have filled them (see above).

Mushroom Ketchup

2kg mushrooms, chopped
50g salt
600ml white vinegar
1 teaspoon freshly ground black peppercorns
½ teaspoon ground ginger
½ teaspoon ground cinnamon
A good pinch of ground nutmeg
3 level teaspoons sugar

1. Place the chopped mushrooms in a shallow dish, sprinkle with the salt, and cover and leave overnight.

2. Rinse and drain the mushrooms and place in a large pan.

3. Add the vinegar, spices and sugar.

4. Cover with a lid and simmer for about 30 minutes.

5. Push through a sieve or blend in a food processor.

6. Heat again in a pan to simmering and then pour into warm bottles and seal.

7. Label and date when cool.

Storage
This should be consumed within 2 weeks if unopened or 5 days once opened. To prolong the life of this ketchup it is advisable to sterilise the bottles (see page 170).

Tomato and Red Pepper Ketchup

MAKES ABOUT 1.5 LITRES

2kg ripe tomatoes, chopped
3 onions, finely chopped
4 red peppers, finely chopped
1.2 litres white vinegar
2 teaspoons salt
1 teaspoon ground ginger
½ teaspoon ground cloves or black peppercorns
1 teaspoon ground allspice
130g soft brown sugar

1. Put all the ingredients in a pan and bring slowly to simmering, stirring constantly.

2. Bring to the boil then simmer for about 45 minutes.

3. Rub the mixture through a sieve and simmer the pulp again for about 10 minutes or until it is a similar consistency to double cream.

4. Pour into warm bottles and seal well.

5. Label and date the bottles when cool.

Storage
This will keep for 4 weeks if kept in the fridge or 7 days once opened. To prolong the life of the ketchup the bottles may be sterilised (see page 170).

Sauces

Rich Tomato Sauce

This recipe has a richer tomato flavour and is slightly spicier than the ketchup, but can be served in the same way. The recipe makes approximately 1.5 litres of sauce and is an excellent way of using up a crop of ripe tomatoes.

MAKES ABOUT 1.5 LITRES

600ml white vinegar
½ teaspoon ground allspice
½ teaspoon ground cinnamon
A pinch of grated nutmeg
3kg ripe tomatoes
25g salt
1 level teaspoon paprika
200g golden caster sugar

1. Put the vinegar in a pan with the spices and bring to the boil then remove from the heat and leave to stand.

2. Wash and slice the tomatoes and place in another pan, preferably a preserving pan. Bring to a simmer and cook for about 15 minutes or until the tomatoes are soft and pulpy. Rub the pulp through a fine sieve and place back in the same pan.

3. Add the salt and paprika and bring to a simmer, stirring occasionally.

4. Add the vinegar and sugar and continue to cook over a medium heat, stirring constantly until all the sugar has dissolved.

5. Simmer the mixture for about 35–40 minutes or until the consistency resembles that of double cream; do not boil as this will affect the flavour. Stir occasionally.

6. Pour into warm bottles leaving a 2cm space at the top and screw on the lids immediately.

7. When cool, label and date the bottles.

Storage
This will keep in the fridge for 4 weeks unopened. Once opened, consume within 7 days. Do not keep the sauce for any longer as it can start to ferment.

Green Tomato Sauce

This is a delicious sauce that can be prepared with those pesky tomatoes that just won't ripen. It is a sweet, mildly spiced sauce that goes well with steaks or burgers.

MAKES ABOUT 500ML

1.5kg under-ripe tomatoes, chopped
2 Bramley or other cooking apples, peeled and chopped
1 small onion, finely chopped
250g white sugar
½ teaspoon ground white pepper
A pinch of ground allspice
1 level teaspoon dry mustard
1 tablespoon salt
280ml malt vinegar

1. Put all the ingredients together in a large pan over a low heat and stir until the sugar has dissolved.

2. Bring to the boil then simmer gently for about 45 minutes until everything is pulpy and soft.

3. Push through a sieve and simmer again in the pan for 5 minutes.

4. Pour the mixture into warm bottles and seal well.

5. Label and date the bottles when cool.

Storage
Sterilise the bottles (see page 170) if you wish to prolong the life of the sauce. Otherwise it should keep for 4 weeks in the fridge unopened. Once opened, consume within 1 week.

Brown Sauce

This is spicy, full-flavoured brown-style sauce, great on chips. The salt and sugar levels can be adjusted to suit your own taste.

MAKES ABOUT 350ML

500g cooking apples, cored and chopped
500g plums, stoned and chopped
1 small onion, chopped
2 cloves garlic, grated
2 level teaspoons salt
500ml malt vinegar
150g dark brown sugar
½ teaspoon each of ground ginger, ground allspice and cayenne pepper

1. Put the fruit, onion and garlic together in a large pan and bring to the boil, then reduce the heat and simmer for about 15 minutes until everything is pulpy.

2. Push the pulp through a sieve and put back in the pan with the salt, vinegar, sugar and spices.

3. Bring to the boil slowly, stirring until the sugar has dissolved. When the mixture is boiling reduce the heat and simmer for about 20 minutes or until it reaches a thick but pourable consistency.

4. Allow to cool for 10 minutes then pour into warm bottles and seal well.

5. Label and date the bottles when cool.

Storage
You can use this as soon as it is cool. Store in a cool, dark place and use within 4 months.

Apple Sauce

This traditional sauce is a wonderful accompaniment to roast pork and goose. But I also like it with some good pork sausages.

MAKES ABOUT 4 X 500G JARS

2kg Bramley or other cooking apples, washed
450ml water plus 100ml extra
2 rounded tablespoons golden granulated sugar
½ level teaspoon ground cinnamon
50g butter

1. Chop the unpeeled apples into small pieces and place in a pan with 450ml of the water, the sugar and cinnamon. Bring to the boil then turn down the heat and simmer until the apples are soft and have fallen. Add the extra water if necessary during this cooking time.

2. Rub the mixture through a sieve and return it to the pan with the butter. Simmer for 5 minutes until thick and pour into warm sterile jars. Seal well.

3. Allow to cool thoroughly then label and date the jars.

Storage
This sauce can be stored for 4 weeks unopened in the fridge. It will also freeze well and can be kept frozen for 6 months.

Mint Sauce

This sauce is a traditional accompaniment to roast lamb. There is generally no point in making this in large quantities as it has a very concentrated flavour so you only need small amounts for any one meal.

MAKES ABOUT 1 X 450G JAR

350ml white vinegar
200g white granulated sugar
100g fresh mint leaves
A pinch of salt

1. Put the vinegar and the sugar in a pan and bring slowly to the boil, stirring constantly until all the sugar dissolves. Continue to boil for a full 5 minutes then remove from the heat.

2. Chop the mint leaves very finely and add to the vinegar with the salt.

3. Bring the mixture back to the boil and stir. Then boil for 2 more minutes.

4. Cool for about 15 minutes then pour into the warm sterile jar and seal.

5. Label and date when cool.

Storage
This should keep for 4–6 months if stored in a cool, dark place. Even after opening it will keep for up to 4 months in the fridge.

Quick Mint Sauce

This recipe is the quickest and longest-lasting version. My grandma used to prepare this and we would have it with Lancashire hotpot as well as lamb chops and roasts. The beauty of it is that you can serve as much or as little as you need.

80g fresh mint leaves
Golden syrup
White wine or malt vinegar to serve

1. Chop the mint leaves very finely and put into a 450g sterile jar. Cover with golden syrup and stir with a sterile spoon.

2. Cover with the lid. The sauce will last all year depending on how often you serve it.

3. When you are ready to serve the mint sauce, mix 1 spoonful of sauce with 1 spoonful of white wine or malt vinegar, whichever you prefer. Stir and serve. Simply measure equal quantities of mint mixture and vinegar. This way you can serve a very small or large amount as you require.

Plum Sauce

This is my favourite sauce to serve with roast duck, but it also goes well with roast turkey or chicken.

MAKES ABOUT 3 x 450G JARS OR BOTTLES

1.5kg plums
350g sugar
700ml malt or white vinegar (malt gives a deeper colour)
1 teaspoon salt
1 teaspoon ground ginger
1 teaspoon ground cinnamon
A pinch of ground cloves

1. Chop the plums and put them in a pan with their stones.

2. Add all the other ingredients and heat, stirring constantly until the sugar has dissolved.

3. Bring to the boil then reduce the heat and simmer for 40 minutes or until the mixture is thick and the plums are pulpy.

4. Rub the mixture through a sieve then return it to the pan.

5. Simmer for 30 more minutes or until the mixture is thick but pourable.

6. Allow to cool for 10 minutes before bottling in warm sterile jars and sealing well. Label and date when cool.

Storage
This will keep for 2 months unopened. It's best to leave the sauce for 4 days before consuming to allow the flavours to develop. Once opened store in the fridge and use within 2 weeks.

Flavoured Vinegars

Many foods can be enhanced by adding a little flavoured vinegar, and none more so than salads. They make an excellent and unusual gift for friends and family.

Fruit vinegars are usually made from soft fruits such as blackberries and raspberries. They can be used to flavour sauces and the sweetened version can be diluted to make a summer drink. A blackcurrant one is ideal if you have a nasty sore throat; it can be diluted with iced water and sipped.

Apart from the storage bottles and funnel you will need a large pot or glass bowl in which to prepare your vinegars and once again a large muslin straining bag or cloth tied around the pan. All the flavoured vinegars will keep for up to 9 months unopened. Once opened, store in the fridge and use within 3 weeks.

How to Prepare Fruit Vinegars

To make unsweetened vinegars
Use 1kg fruit to every litre of white wine vinegar. Blackcurrants, red and white currants, raspberries, strawberries and blackberries are ideal either as single fruits or as part of a mixture.

To make sweetened vinegars
You will need a 2-litre jug to measure the vinegar.

1. Wash the fruit well and drain.

2. Put the fruit into a large clean bowl.

3. Use the back of a wooden spoon to squash the fruit slightly.

4. Pour over the vinegar.

5. Cover with a cloth and leave to stand for 4 days. Stir once a day.

6. Strain the vinegar into a pan and bring to the boil.

7. Boil for 10 minutes. Cool slightly and pour into warm sterile bottles.

Follow steps 1–5 of the unsweetened version then:

6. Measure the amount of vinegar you have and pour into a pan.

7. For every 100ml of vinegar use 100g sugar for a syrup-type vinegar or 50g for a lighter vinegar and stir into the fruit vinegar in the pan.

8. Stir over a low heat until the sugar has dissolved then bring to the boil and continue to boil for 10 minutes.

9. Cool slightly before pouring into warm sterile bottles.

How to Prepare Herb Vinegars

These make excellent salad and vegetable dressings, and can be added to soups and stews to give depth to the flavour. Always start with a small amount though, and taste before adding more. Use thyme, tarragon, mint, dill, marjoram, rosemary or a combination for this recipe.
If you are using mint leaves, chop them before adding to the vinegar. For other herbs bruise the leaves with the back of a wooden spoon or a large pestle.

1. Use a litre-sized jar and fill to at least a third full with clean fresh herb leaves; the more you use the more concentrated will be the flavour of the vinegar.

2. Top up with white wine vinegar, leaving about 2cm at the top of the jar.

3. Cover with the lid and leave in a cool, dark place for 3–4 weeks.

4. Strain the vinegar and either pour back into the jar or into warm sterile bottles.

5. Add a sprig of whatever herb you have used to the finished vinegar.

To make garlic vinegar
Add 75g thinly sliced fresh garlic cloves to 1 litre white vinegar and cover well and leave for 2–3 weeks. Strain into bottles.

To make chilli vinegar
Split 50g of red chillies down the centre and place in a litre jar. Pour over any kind of vinegar and seal well. Leave to steep for 4–5 weeks. Strain into bottles.

To make horseradish vinegar
1. Grate 80g horseradish into a litre jar and add 2 finely chopped shallots. Top up with either malt or white vinegar.

2. Seal the jar and leave for about 12 days, giving the jar a shake once or twice.

3. Strain into warm sterile jars or bottles.

12. Making Fruit Syrups

Syrups are quite easy to make but do take a little time. They are worth the effort though if you like authentic, fresh, fruity flavours. Because there is no boiling in the preparation of the syrups they do have a limited shelf life, especially the less sweet ones. So storing them in the fridge is a necessity to keep them as fresh as possible for the longest period of time. See each individual recipe for details of how long each syrup will keep.

Points to remember when making syrups

- Use only perfect ripe fruit for the best flavour.
- Never boil the fruit or syrup as this will impair the flavour.
- Only use white sugar as this gives the purest flavour and clearest syrup.

Equipment for making syrups

You will need the following equipment for making syrups:

- a large pan and a large heat-resistant glass or earthenware bowl that fits comfortably inside as with a double boiler;
- a wooden spoon;
- a muslin or jelly bag;
- a 2-litre measuring jug;
- sterilised bottles with well-fitting lids;
- a funnel to help with filling the bottles;
- a ladle.

How to Make Fruit Syrups

1. Prepare the fruit

Use ripe and juicy-looking fruit for the best results; those that have become too ripe for jam-making are ideal for syrups. Wash the fruit in cold water and discard any bad ones.

2. Heat the fruit

Place the fruit in the bowl and mash with the back of a wooden spoon; this helps release the juice quickly and thus retain the flavour. Some fruits will need the addition of water:

blackberries – 100ml water for every kilo of fruit;
blackcurrants – 280ml water for every kilo of fruit;
loganberries, raspberries and strawberries need no water adding;
redcurrants – 150ml water for every kilo of fruit.

Fill the large pan with hot water and heat to simmering. Place the bowl of fruit in the pan and heat without stirring until the juices begin to run, then mash the fruit again. Heat for another 5 minutes and mash again. This ensures the optimum amount of juice will be extracted from the fruit.

3. Strain the juice

Pour the contents of the bowl into a muslin or jelly bag and hang over a large bowl to catch the juice. Two layers of muslin can be made into a bag if you don't have a jelly bag. Leave overnight. Unlike the process of making jellies, when squeezing the bag spoils the clarity of the preserve, it is quite acceptable the next day to squeeze the bag to extract as much as possible of the juice that is left. Measure the juice in the jug ready to weigh the sugar.

4. Add the sugar

Using white caster sugar helps speed up the dissolving time, but white granulated is also fine. Other sugars spoil the true fruit flavour of the syrups.

For a sweet, thick syrup that is ideal for topping desserts and ice creams, allow 300g sugar for every 500ml juice. This syrup has the longest shelf life and will keep for up to 2 months in the fridge. It can also be diluted for drinks.

For a less sweet syrup that is ideal for everyday drinks diluted to taste and for ice lollies, use 200g sugar for every 500ml juice. This will keep for up to 3 weeks in the fridge. The best dilution for lollies is to use half syrup to half water.

For a tangy syrup that is great for people who prefer less sweetness, and good for drinks, cocktails and anything you fancy, use 100g sugar to 500ml juice. This will keep for 7–10 days in the fridge.

Stir the sugar into the juice without heating. The more concentrated syrups may need to be placed over a bowl of hot water to help the sugar dissolve completely, but if you are patient it will happen.

5. Bottle the syrup

Ladle the juice into sterile bottles using a funnel to help prevent spillages. Make sure the lids are tightly screwed on immediately. Label and date the bottles.

To prolong the shelf life of syrups, they can be sterilised as described in Chapter 11, page 170, for ketchups and sauces.

As an alternative to the heat method of sterilisation, you can add one Campden tablet crushed in a tablespoon of cool boiled water to the syrup before bottling and stir it in until it dissolves. One Campden tablet will sterilise up to 1 litre of syrup. But this can sometimes cause the colour of the syrups to fade over a few days, spoiling the look of them. I find it best just to use up the syrups quickly; this is no hardship as they are so delicious everyone will want some!

You can now enjoy your syrups straight away. If the juice has been standing for any length of time, sediment will form at the bottom of the syrups. This is nothing to worry about; it is only particles of fruit that have been suspended in the juice. If you prefer not to have this in your syrup, either be careful not to shake the bottle before pouring it out or strain the syrup again before bottling. Otherwise just shake up the bottle, pour and enjoy.

13. Recipes Using Your Preserves

Preserves can be used in so many ways: from filling jam tarts to thickening and enriching sauces and gravies. This chapter is all about the many ways they can be used – and hopefully will inspire you to be creative with your own lovingly prepared jars and bottles of preserves.

Using Jams

A Victoria sandwich cake is perfectly complemented by a thick spreading of raspberry jam, but it can be equally delicious filled with other types of jam – never mind WI regulations!

Simple Jam Tarts

A simple jam tart was always my children's favourite treat; they would choose a home-made tart over a chocolate biscuit. Jam tarts can be made quickly when you need them, and if you have some pastry in the freezer it's even easier, so long as you remember to defrost it.

Just roll out the pastry to about 4mm thick and cut to size with a pastry cutter. Remember that pastry shrinks when it's cooked so make sure your pastry shells come well up the sides of your well-greased bun or tart tins.

A small teaspoon of your chosen jam, marmalade or lemon or orange curd is about right as the filling soon bubbles over and tends to stick to the tray if you're not careful. Cook for about 10–12 minutes at 190°C/gas mark 5. Remember the filling will be very hot when you take the tarts out of the oven so cool them a little before eating. We make lots of different flavours and they keep well in an airtight tin.

Variation

Try a similar tart but on a larger scale. Roll out your pastry to fit an 18cm round sandwich-type tin and fill with jam or whatever you fancy. I prefer making one of these with mincemeat at Christmas and topping with a lattice of pastry. This saves a bit of time when there are so many other things to do. It also means you get more mincemeat than pastry with every bite! Cooking time needs to be extended to about 25–30 minutes for this larger tart.

Apple Meringue Pie

This makes a change from lemon meringue pie.

300g shortcrust pastry
4 tablespoons dessert apple jam
1 large Bramley apple
A squeeze of lemon juice
2 egg whites
80g caster sugar

1. Preheat the oven to 190°C/gas mark 5 and grease a 20cm round baking tin or deep pie dish.

2. Roll out the pastry to about 4mm thick and use it to line the prepared dish. Bake the pastry blind for about 20 minutes. Cool for 10 minutes.

3. Spread the base of the pastry case evenly with the apple jam.

4. Peel, core and slice the apple thinly and squeeze a little lemon juice over it.

5. Arrange the apples in the jam concentrically.

6. Whisk the egg whites until stiff then add half of the sugar and whisk for a few seconds. Fold in the rest of the sugar with a metal spoon.

7. Spoon the meringue over the apples to cover, taking it right to the edge of the pastry shell.

8. Bake for 20 minutes until the meringue is golden brown. Serve with cream when just cool.

Jam Rings

These are very similar to jammy dodger biscuits. They are easy to make and fun for children to make with you. Try using a few different-flavoured jams to fill the biscuits.

MAKES ABOUT 15 BISCUITS

200g butter, softened to room temperature
150g golden granulated sugar
2 egg yolks, beaten
½–1 teaspoon vanilla extract
225g plain flour
80g ground almonds
Jam to fill the biscuit

1. Preheat the oven to 180°C/gas mark 4 and grease 2 baking sheets.

2. Cream the butter and sugar together until it is light and fluffy and beat in the egg yolks and vanilla extract.

3. Sift in the flour and sprinkle over the ground almonds. Stir in with a metal spoon.

4. Bring the dough together with your hands.

5. Use half of the dough and roll out to about 3mm thick. Cut out circles with a biscuit cutter and lay them on one of the baking sheets.

6. Roll out the second half of the dough and again cut out circles with the biscuit cutter. Then use a very small cutter to cut circles out of the centre of this second batch, so that you are left with rings. Lay these on the second tray.

7. Bake for about 15 minutes until light golden brown. Cool completely.

8. Spread the jam over the whole circles and sandwich together with the rings on top. To finish, dust with a little icing sugar if you wish.

Variations
For a clear and smooth filling use your jellies to fill the biscuits, or try some tangy lemon curd.

Gooseberry Roly-poly

An easy, comforting pudding to serve on a cold day.

200g self-raising flour
A pinch of salt
25g golden caster sugar
100g vegetarian suet (or the original if you prefer)
4–5 tablespoons water to make a soft but rollable dough
5 tablespoons gooseberry jam

1. Preheat the oven to 200°C/gas mark 6 and grease a baking sheet.

2. Sift the flour and salt together and stir in the sugar and suet.

3. Add 4 tablespoons of the water and stir with a knife to distribute the water evenly. Add the other tablespoon of water if it is needed and bring the dough together with your hands.

4. Roll out onto a lightly floured surface to make a large rectangle about 4mm thick.

5. Spread the jam over the pastry, leaving a 2cm edge of pastry free of jam down one of the long sides.

6. Brush the free edge with water or milk to make a seal and then begin to roll the opposite long side containing jam towards the free edge. Roll the dough right up to the free edge and press down gently to firm the seal. If you like a shiny finish to the pastry you can brush a little beaten egg over the top of the roly-poly and sprinkle with a little brown sugar.

7. Place on the baking sheet and bake for 30–40 minutes, turning the heat down to 180°C/gas mark 4 halfway through the cooking time.

8. When the roly-poly is cooked, allow to rest for 10 minutes then serve with custard.

Variation
Try making this roly-poly with the Winter Conserve in Chapter 8, 'Making Special Preserves' (page 109), instead of the gooseberry jam.

Soufflé Jam Omelette

This can be eaten as a dessert or makes a lovely supper dish when you fancy something sweet. It can be served with any flavour jam you like.

SERVES 4 AS A DESSERT OR 2 AS A SUPPER DISH

4 eggs, separated
20g caster sugar
A pinch of salt
2 heaped tablespoons jam
25g butter

1. Preheat the grill and have ready a piece of foil or greaseproof paper sprinkled with a little caster sugar.

2. Beat the egg yolks and sugar together in a bowl.

3. Whisk the egg whites with the salt until stiff and place the jam in a small pan over a very low heat to warm and melt.

4. Melt the butter in a large flat-based frying pan or omelette pan.

5. Fold the egg whites into the beaten egg yolk mixture, and when the butter is very hot pour in the egg mixture and cook for about 3 minutes.

6. Put the pan under the grill and the mixture will rise up and turn golden brown. This should take about 2 minutes.

7. Slide the omelette onto the foil or paper and spread the jam over the grilled surface. Use the foil to help fold the omelette in half and slide carefully onto a warmed plate. Serve immediately.

Using Jellies

These can be used to great effect as glazes when you are roasting meats. Glazes enhance the flavour of meat and give it a shiny or sticky finish.

For beef and venison – brush the joint of meat with blackberry jelly just before cooking and add a little more halfway through.

For lamb – brush redcurrant jelly onto the joint before cooking and add a little more during cooking to enhance the flavour of the meat and the gravy.

For chicken drumsticks or thighs – glaze with cranberry jelly to give a sticky yet tangy flavour.

For goose – gooseberry jelly is ideal to brush over the skin and stir into the gravy. I wonder if that is where the fruit gets its name?

For pork – obviously apple jelly is wonderful, but try it with redcurrant or cranberry for a change.

For hams – coat a partly boiled ham with orange jelly and sprinkle a very small amount of ground cinnamon over it and then roast. This makes an easy and very seasonal-flavoured Christmas ham.

Use the jellies to thicken and flavour gravies and sauces. Try the following recipe.

Cumberland Sauce

This is a luxurious sauce that can make a simple dish into something very special. It makes an excellent accompaniment to game dishes or hot and cold hams, but I think it's also great with pork sausages and mashed potatoes. It will keep in a sterilised jar for 8 weeks in the fridge, so make double and have some ready for next time.

SERVES 4

200g redcurrant jelly
150ml port
Grated zest and juice of 1 lemon
Grated zest and juice of 1 orange
A pinch of cayenne pepper
2 teaspoons Worcestershire sauce

1. Put the redcurrant jelly in a pan over a very low heat until the jelly melts.

2. Stir in the port and bring to the boil, stirring occasionally.

3. Reduce the heat to simmering and continue to cook until the mixture has reduced by a third and is beginning to thicken.

4. Remove from the heat and stir in the other ingredients. Mix well together and allow to cool.

Serving
Serve hot or cold depending on the meat you are serving it with. The sauce may be reheated if necessary, but heat gently without boiling.

When you have made fruit tarts, use a little warmed jelly to glaze the tops of the fruit before serving.

Jellies can also be used as hot sauces to top steamed and sponge puddings and ice creams.

Raspberry Ripple Ice Cream

This is easiest made in an ice-cream maker, but if you don't have one it can be done by hand. Make sure your freezer is on its coldest setting before you begin. Store the ice cream in a large freezable container that has a well-fitting lid.

MAKES ABOUT 800G

For the ice cream
250ml single cream
250ml double cream
100ml milk
3 tablespoons raspberry jelly
4 egg yolks
100g caster sugar

For the ripple
200g fresh raspberries
150g raspberry jelly

1. Put the creams and milk into a pan with the jelly and bring slowly to boiling point, stirring gently with a wooden spoon. Remove from the heat.

2. Beat the egg yolks and sugar together in a bowl.

3. Pour over the cream mixture, stirring constantly, and return the mixture to the pan.

4. Heat gently over a medium heat until the custard thickens. Don't let it boil or it will separate and spoil.

5. Whisk well for a few seconds then allow to cool.

6. Meanwhile put the raspberries and jelly in a pan over a low heat and mash the fruit into the melting jelly. Heat until the jelly has melted and then allow to cool.

7. If you have an ice-cream maker use it to freeze the custard following the manufacturer's instructions. Add the ripple sauce close to the end of the freezing time while the ice cream is still churning. Be careful not to let it churn too much.

8. To make the ice cream by hand whisk the custard for a few seconds then pour into a freezable container and place in the freezer for 30 minutes. Then remove from the freezer and break up the ice crystals that have formed. Repeat the process and this time swirl in the ripple as you break up the crystals. Leave to freeze completely. How long this takes will depend on your freezer.

Using Curds

Lemon, orange and apricot curds are useful for filling sandwich cakes and Swiss rolls. Try making some simple sponge buns and cutting the tops out as you would for butterfly buns but, rather than spooning in buttercream, put a teaspoon of curd on the buns and replace the tops. Dust with icing sugar or glacé icing.

When you are making a cheesecake add 2–3 tablespoons of lemon curd to the cheese mixture for a lemony flavoured finish.

Lemon Crunch Biscuits

These have an attractive crackly top and melt in the mouth.

MAKES ABOUT 15 BISCUITS

230g plain flour
2 level teaspoons baking powder
A pinch of salt
2 level teaspoons ground ginger
120g butter
100g caster sugar
3 tablespoons golden syrup
2–3 tablespoons lemon curd

1. Preheat the oven to 200°C/gas mark 6 and grease a large baking sheet or 2 smaller ones.

2. Sieve the flour, baking powder, salt and ginger into a mixing bowl.

3. Rub the butter into the flour.

4. Stir in the sugar, pour in the golden syrup and add 1 tablespoon of the lemon curd. Mix thoroughly with a wooden spoon and bring together with your hands to make a dough.

5. Using lightly floured hands, roll the dough into small balls and place on a baking sheet making sure the balls have enough room to spread out; about 2cm is probably sufficient.

6. Press lightly down in the centre of each ball with your finger and place a drop of lemon curd in the little dip; about one third of a teaspoon should be enough.

7. Bake for about 10–12 minutes, keeping an eye on the biscuits so they don't burn. They should be a deep golden colour.

8. Leave to cool on a wire rack.

Using Special Preserves

Apple and Mincemeat Crumble

This makes a change from an apple crumble and is a way of using up any spare mincemeat after Christmas. I find this is sweet enough without adding any more sugar to the apples, but, if you prefer it sweeter, sprinkle a tablespoon of soft brown sugar over the apples before adding the crumble.

SERVES 4

4 tablespoons mincemeat (any will do)
250g plain flour
50g porridge oats
180g butter
180g unrefined caster sugar
2 large Bramley apples

1. Preheat the oven to 200°C/gas mark 6 and butter a deep pie dish.

2. Spread the mincemeat evenly over the bottom of the dish.

3. Sift the flour into a bowl and stir in the oats.

4. Rub in the butter until the mixture looks like breadcrumbs.

5. Stir in the sugar.

6. Peel, core and slice the apples and place the slices on top of the mincemeat.

7. Sprinkle over the crumble topping so that it covers the filling evenly.

8. Bake for 25–30 minutes or until the crumble is golden in colour.

9. Serve hot or cold with cream or custard.

Chocolate and Cherry Layer Cake

This is an easy-to-make cake that is great for a celebration meal.
The cake can be made 1–2 days before it is needed and kept in an
airtight tin before filling.

SERVES 8

180g butter
180g soft brown sugar
200g self-raising flour
3 eggs, beaten
30g cocoa
50g dark chocolate, melted
2 tablespoons milk
4 tablespoons cherry brandy
4 tablespoons black cherry conserve
100ml whipping cream
100g dark chocolate, melted, for the top
Fresh dark cherries to decorate

1. Preheat the oven to 170°C/gas mark 3 and grease and line a 450g loaf tin.

2. Cream the butter and sugar together until light and fluffy.

3. Sift in 1 tablespoon of the flour and beat in the eggs.

4. Sift the flour and cocoa into the creamed mixture and fold in with a metal spoon.

5. Fold in the 50g melted chocolate and the milk.

6. Spoon into the prepared tin and smooth out the top, making a dip in the centre to avoid the middle rising more than the rest of the cake.

7. Bake for 40 minutes then turn the oven down to 150°C/gas mark 2 and cook for a further 20 minutes. Test to see if the centre is cooked by inserting a skewer into the cake. If it comes out clean the cake is cooked; if any mixture sticks to the skewer, cook for a further 10 minutes.

8. Cool in the tin for 15 minutes then transfer to a wire rack. Leave to cool completely before adding the filling.

Serving
When the cake is cool, slice into 3 equal layers and sprinkle each layer with a little cherry brandy – not too much or the cake will be difficult to serve. Spread 2 tablespoons each of the cherry conserve over the bottom two sections. Whip the cream until it holds its shape and spread over the conserve. Place the layers carefully on top of one another. Spread the chocolate over the top and finish with some fresh dark cherries.

Using Chutneys, Relishes and Pickles

For a delicious toasty treat, toast some bread, butter it to your taste, spread with one of your home-made chutneys or relishes and top with some mature Cheddar cheese. Pop under the grill for 5 minutes or until the cheese is bubbling. Eat with care – the chutney gets very hot under the cheese.

Pork and Pickle Lattice Pie

This is an excellent slicing pie for buffets and picnics.

SERVES 10

For the hot water crust pastry
500g plain flour
1 level teaspoon salt
1 level teaspoon dry mustard
220g lard
220ml hot water

For the filling
1kg minced pork
1 level teaspoon salt
½ teaspoon white pepper
3–4 tablespoons brown-style pickle or one of the apple chutneys

1. Preheat the oven to 180°C/gas mark 4.

2. Grease a 20cm loose-bottomed deep round cake tin.

3. Sieve the flour, salt and mustard together into a bowl.

4. Make a well in the centre.

5. Melt the lard in the hot water and when it is completely melted stir into the flour to make a dough. Bring together with your hands and knead to make a pliable dough.

6. Allow to cool before using.

7. Roll out ½ of the dough and line the prepared tin.

8. Put the meat into a bowl, sprinkle with the salt and pepper and mix well with your hands to distribute the seasoning. Pack half of the meat into the pastry shell and press down evenly.

9. Spread the pickle or chutney over the top of this layer of meat.

10. Press the rest of the meat on the top of the pickle/chutney layer. Roll out the rest of the pastry, cut into thin strips and form a lattice lid on top of the pie. Wet the edges of the strips just before you attach them to the edges of the base and press the two together. If you have a lattice cutter this job is much easier. Brush the top with an egg wash if you like a shiny-topped pie.

11. Place the tin on a baking sheet to make it easier to carry it in and out of the oven and to catch any stray drips of juice from the pie.

12. Bake for 1½ hours then test the centre with a skewer to see if it is cooked; the skewer should come out clean of mixture. If it needs extra cooking time, pop back in the oven and cook for 15 minutes longer.

Burger Surprises

To add flavour to your burgers, when forming the meat patties add a teaspoon of chutney to the centre of the burger and fold the meat around it to encase. Fry them as you would normally. Tomato-based chutneys are great with beef, apple-based chutneys with pork, and red onion chutney is amazing in the centre of lamb burgers.

Tangy Cheese Tarts

When making cheese tarts, dot some tomato or red onion chutney over the pastry shell before sprinkling over the cheese. Crumbly cheeses such as Lancashire or Cheshire are particularly good for this.

Quick Barbecue Sauce

This is great for coating pork chops or chicken drumsticks prior to cooking in the oven or on the barbecue

1 tablespoon sunflower oil
3 tablespoons home-made tomato ketchup
2 teaspoons honey or golden syrup
3 cloves garlic, grated
1 tablespoon soy sauce
1 tablespoon balsamic vinegar

1. Whisk all the ingredients together and use to coat your meat.

2. Allow to marinate for a couple of hours in the fridge before cooking.

Index

Lightning Source UK Ltd.
Milton Keynes UK
UKHW020806120920
369796UK00009B/438